♫ TOM

Tom Russell may be the last of our pioneering western creatives. A renaissance artist, he is at once a singer/songwriter, painter and essayist. His words can sting with the truth, but are always welcome gifts—"palabras de santo, unas le gato" ("Words of a saint, nails of a cat").

—**Bill Reynolds,** Publisher of *Ranch & Reata*,
former Associate Publisher of *Cowboys & Indians*

Tom Russell has made his mark as one of the most distinguished and unconventional singer-songwriters in the Western genre. A master at musical narratives, he captivates audiences with his timeless tunes about the West, and strikes a rich chord with contemporary cowboys who appreciate his authenticity, grittiness and restless spirit.

—**Jennifer Denison,** Senior Editor, *Western Horseman*

An artist in every sense of the word, Tom Russell puts words into art, art into music, and music of the West into your soul. Nobody else in the world can do the West as Tom does.

—**C.J. Hadley,** publisher, *RANGE*

The beautiful thing about a Tom Russell song is that each line feels as honestly earned and perfectly located as the sun-hewn furrows on a rancher's face. Russell has been writing and recording since the early 1970s and has covered a lot of musical ground in that time, but he's arguably at his best when writing about cowboys and about the West.

—**Tom Wilmes,** *American Cowboy*

Tom Russell's songs count in a sea of songs that don't count for much. The reason is both craft and a strong sense of the epic, the heroic, those things that put us humans on the line. And it's those song lines from the front lines of life that make Tom a great songwriter.

—**Hal Cannon,** Founding Director, Western Folklife Center

Russell's *Man from God* is a massive work of guts and grace . . .
—*Time Out,* London-New York

Russell's *Man From God* summons the spirit of Walt Whitman's *Leaves of Grass* . . . Russell's reach is both wide and deep, balancing the grand sweep of history with the individual histories of his ancestors.

—**Charles M. Young,** *The Atlantic* Monthly

Like Carl Sandburg, Russell has honored the painful birthing of early and twentieth century America . . . a brutal honesty and tenderness sets his songs apart.

—*True West*

Tom Russell brings us right into the scene. Bloodcurdling! You can smell the smoke.

—Ramblin' Jack Elliott

Tom Russell is the finest writer of gothic western music.

—Ian Tyson

Tom Russell writes better songs than most anyone . . . but the songs about his own blood country, his heritage, and the magic rangeland of men on horseback affect me like wonderful novels. There is plot, character, passion, and resolution . . . he is an artist.

—Buck Ramsey

Tom Russell is the best songwriter alive and well in the near, far, and middle West. I am blessed to know him and record his fine tunes

—Katie Lee

If America needs an heir to Johnny Cash, Tom Russell just might be the man. He's the real deal.

—Uncut

Tom Russell is an original, a brilliant songwriter with a restless curiosity and an almost violent imagination . . .

—Annie Prouxl

How great is Tom Russell? Isn't he the best? I'd like to quit my job and travel with him . . . if the money can be worked out.

—David Letterman

Russell's *Man From God* should be required listening for every student of American history . . . one of the most important folk records ever recorded.

—John Lomax III

The greatest living folk-country songwriter is a man named Tom Russell. He's written songs that capture the essence of America. A trait that can only be matched by the country's greatest novelists . . .

—John Swenson, *Rolling Stone*

The best songwriter of the generation following Bob Dylan . . .

—Mike Regenstreif, Montreal *Gazette*

Tom Russell is Johnny Cash, Jim Harrison and Charles Bukowski rolled into one. I feel a great affinity with Tom Russell's songs, for he is writing out of the wounded heart of America.

—Lawrence Ferlinghetti

THE ROSE OF ROSCRAE

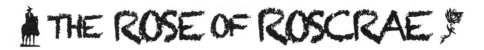

THE ROSE OF ROSCRAE

A BALLAD OF THE WEST

TOM RUSSELL

PROGRAM GUIDE with LIBRETTO

FRONTERA PRESS
Kansas City, Missouri

Frontera Press, a division of Frontera Records
P.O. Box 5933, Kansas City, Missouri 64171-0933

www.fronterarecords.com

10 9 8 7 6 5 4 3 2 1

ISBN: 978-1-4951-3923-9

Song Credits

Words and Music by Thomas George Russell (Frontera Music, ASCAP, Bug/BMG) except:

The Rose of Roscrae (Thomas George Russell/Gretchen Peters/Barry Walsh: Frontera Music, ASCAP, Bug/BMG; Barry
Walsh Music, ASCAP; Circus Girl Music/Carnival Girl Music, ASCAP), The Last Running (Lyrics: Russell, Music: 'I Will Be
Standing' by John Platania/Chip Taylor, Black Road Music, BMI), The Ballad of William Sycamore (Stephen Vincent Benet),
Home On The Range (Lyrics: Higley, Music: Traditional), America (Walt Whitman), Just A Closer Walk With Thee (Unknown,
added rap by Tom Russell), The Road To Fairfax County (David Massengill, David Massengill Music, ASCAP), Blood On
The Saddle (Everett Cheetham, BMI), The Juice of the Barley (Traditional, Irish names by Tom Russell), Sonora's Death
Row (Blackie Farrell, Drifter Music/Bug Music, BMI), The Castration Of The Strawberry Roan (Curley Fletcher), The Door
Song (Crow), Crazy Horse (John Trudell, Poet Tree Publishing, ASCAP), Custer's Luck (Thad Beckman, BMI), Rock of Ages
(Augustus Toplady), When The Wolves No Longer Sing (Tom Russell/Ian Tyson, Frontera Music, ASCAP/Slick Fork Music,
ASCAP), Jesus Met The Woman At The Well (Traditional, arr. Ian & Sylvia), En Canadiene Errant (Gerin-Lajoie), Doin' Hard
Time In Texas (Maxfield, Russell), Western Cowboy (Ledbetter), Desperados Waiting For A Train (Guy Clark, administered
by Alfred Publishing Co.), Tularosa (Thomas George Russell/Gretchen Peters/Barry Walsh: Frontera Music, ASCAP, Bug/
BMG; Barry Walsh Music, ASCAP; Circus Girl Music/Carnival Girl Music, ASCAP)

Traditional: Bury Me Not On The Lone Prairie, Streets of Laredo, Red River Valley, Goodbye Old Paint, Sam Hall, St. James
Hospital, Ain't No More Cane On The Brazos, The Unfortunate Rake, Carrickfergus, The Water Is Wide, The Man Who Rode
The Mule Around The World, Old Desert Sands, The Railroad Boy, Irish Medley, Isn't It Grand?

❧ CONTENTS ❧

Preface . . . .   *ix*

Acknowledgments . . . .   *xi*

Dedication . . . .   *xiii*

Synopsis Act One   1

Synopsis Act Two   3

The Complete Lyrical Ballad, Act One   5

The Complete Lyrical Ballad, Act Two   27

Notes On The Songs   45

The Performers   67

Epilogue   81

Preface:
The Rose of Roscrae

Am I doomed to wander through all eternities?
Don Quixote on a bone spavined nag?

—Irish Johnny Dutton

IN THE 1970S workers tearing down the fun house at the Long Beach Pike, near where I grew up in L.A., discovered a dummy on the wall—which turned out to be the mummified remains of an old gunfighter. Could this be our Johnny Behind-the-Deuce? It got me to thinkin' . . .

What's going on here? A Broadway show? And what's the story? It's the *songs* we recall from musicals, isn't it? A Ballad of the West? A Folk Opera? We have a deep yen in this country to name things and categorize them. Listen to the record and decide for yourself, but if you care to go down the rabbit hole a bit further I'll add some of my thoughts.

Maybe this is *Les Miserables* with cowboy hats. Try to figure out the plot to *Les Miserables*, the musical. It's a bit unfathomable and complex. A second level French Revolution and complicated love intrigues and war and poverty and so on, and a lawman chasing an ex-con (we have that in ours, too) but it's the songs that rise above it all. How does it end? I can't remember. I can sing you two or three of the songs, though. And every word of dialogue is sung. Is that an opera?

I can only tell you how this idea for a show began and how it ended up. Like a painting, it took on its own thrust and coloring. The *voices* took over. And maybe one day it will hit Broadway. That's why I put a dance number in. But onward, to the story background.

I come from horse people. Twenty years ago I began writing songs and filming interviews with my sister-in-law, Claudia Russell, who at the time was ranching alone on a three thousand acre spread in the heart of historic Spanish Land Grant ranching valley in California.

A good portion of the tale had to do with my cowboy brother, who had run off to another relationship—and Claudia's feelings about all this: men, horses, ranching, survival, and the deep history of her family going back many generations from the Carissa Plains to Texas. Pilgrims and hardscrabble ranchers. And, yes, as in our story, Claudia was forced to shoot two bears that had broken into her ranch house kitchen and bedroom. Out there alone, thirty miles from town.

Some of the dialogue in these songs and soliloquies were taken directly from Claudia and my brother Pat: Claudia's story about how to follow game trail to water and about shooting the bears, and Pat's recipe for cooking a ribeye steak. And other lines.

The film on Claudia has never come into focus, as yet, but there were dozens of songs which became the forerunner to the songs on this record. I began toying with the idea of an outlaw nicknamed Johnny Behind-the-Deuce (the name of a real historic character who hung out in Tombstone) but our Johnny is a different breed all together.

By the time I wrote "The Rose of Roscrae" song, with Gretchen Peters and Barry Walsh, I realized I had a larger theme—the Irish kid migrating to America to become a cowboy. His vision of the Last Frontier and his lifelong love/hate relationship with Rose. The "opera" is formed around Johnny, 90 years of age, looking back on his life in the West.

I also wanted to include traditional cowboy music and singers whose voices moved me. *Important* singers—from Finbar Furey to Ramblin' Jack Elliot to Ana Gabriel to Ian Tyson and on and on. I was also interested in finding out and sometimes showing (in song collage), rather then telling, where these traditional songs come from.

Thus the backdrop became a small history of cowboy song; all those voices you hear around the campfire. And then there's the spiritual side of the story with St. Damien and Joseph Dutton, and Johnny's odyssey and such. The long trail toward redemption. It surprises me, as I listen to the mixes, of how many of the songs deal with the spiritual side of things—and trouble, chaos, forgiveness, and resurrection. So be it. The voices seized the moment and I just hung on. Maybe the voices are telling me something I blocked out.

In the end I wanted a show that rang with more "cowboy truth" than the Frontier Musicals I grew up with as a kid: *Oklahoma, Annie Get Your Gun, Calamity Jane* and the like. I loved these shows, and the songs were *big* and enduring, but they were composed and written by professional songwriting Easterners and Tin Pan Alley folk whose views of the West were from afar, and the lyrics sometimes edged into being corny. Even Cole Porter and Johnny Mercer wrote Western songs ("Don't Fence Me In" and "I'm An Old Cowhand From the Rio Grande"—classics!) but written from a far off, romanticized viewpoint.

Enough said. Below, the nuts and bolts of the story and a bit of background on the songs and singers. Be careful down there in the rabbit hole, you might emerge bow-legged, chewing Red Man tobacco, with a chunk missing out of your left ear.

Tom and Pat Russell

❧ ACKNOWLEDGMENTS ❦

So many of my musical heroes lent a hand to this project that it's hard to single out any of them. It starts with Ian and Ramblin' Jack, but snowballs from there to each and every one of the incredibly talented musicians on the record, especially Barry Walsh for his invaluable co-production.

Bill Reynolds designed the cover. I wanted to combine the Western movie poster tradition with a Broadway show vibe, and he did a great job of evoking that "Saul Bass" feel, reminiscent of the Bass film posters for *Vertigo* and *The Man With The Golden Arm*.

Thanks also go to John Yuelkenbeck at Frontera for his editing assistance on this book. John's graphic company, Alias Creative Group, provided the CD and book design/layout.

Corky Carrel and Bill Lavery deserve a hand for the many years they spent distributing my work. And a nod to Jon Polk and Ed "Digger" Becker who have supported me from further back than I care to recall.

Nadine takes care of the business end of things both at home and on the road.

❦ DEDICATION ❦

For Nadine, with love.

Claudia Russell, Pat Russell, St. Damien of Molokai, Joseph Dutton, Marjorie Malloy Russell, and Aunt Mary Russell of Templemore, Ireland—cowboys we shall always be!

Synopsis Act One:
On the trail of the last outlaw

There's a time to cut the wild dogs loose
   —Irish John Dutton

Cowboys we are, cowboys we shall always be
   —Pancho Villa

IT IS SOMETIME in the late 1880s. Sixteen-year-old Johnny Dutton is walking the road from Roscrea, Ireland, back to his home in Templemore. It's late at night and he's just had the "holy shite" beaten out of him by his girlfriend's father, in a stable in Roscrea. Johnny was caught kissing and rolling in the hay with the old man's daughter, the beautiful fifteen-year-old Rose Malloy.

Bleeding and broken-hearted, he vows to flee Ireland, sail to America, become a cowboy and an outlaw and show all the bloody bastards! (Although relatively uneducated and mildly dyslexic, young John has read all the dime novels, you see.) He sneaks a secret note to his Rose of "Roscrae" and gets her promise they'll meet in America, and off he goes, stowing aboard a tramp steamer in Cork. "Roscrea" is forever misspelled in his jangled mind.

Johnny arrives and makes his way across the last frontier and gains employment as a young wrangler for Charles Goodnight, on a ranch in West Texas. There young John witnesses the last Buffalo running of the Comanche. He buys a pistol and disappears into the West, an outlaw for to be!

Our horse opera opens *in medias res,* with Johnny on the gallows, in the midst of his life as a gunslinger and wanderer, minstrel, and fairground pugilist on the last frontier. He's now known as Johnny Behind-the-Deuce, Irish John, and other outlaw handles.

Johnny proceeds to sing us through his life in the West, slices of time and songs heard and sung. He's looking back on 90-odd years. His mind is all jigsawed up with these fragments, due to his age and time as a carnival boxer. He knows a man is seen in fragments, like the descriptions of outlaws on old wanted posters. His mind is addled in fugue states of reasoning. He wants to put the pieces back together—he's carried along by the old songs.

Johnny is about to be hung for a half dozen horses he claimed he didn't steal. He's killed men, but only when they showed him disrespect. He escapes the gallows with the help of the corrupt Judge Squig (played by David Olney). He flees across the frontier with Marshal Augie Blood (played by Augie Meyers) on his trail. Augie Blood thinks Johnny has impregnated his (Augie's) young daughter, and so he trumps up a dozen extra charges, and promises he'll bring Johnny to justice.

Augie Blood is also an evangelistic preacher who travels in a covered wagon pulled by four gospel mules: Mathew, Mark, Luke, and John. Augie has a small upright saloon piano in the back of the wagon, and accompanies himself as he sings old hymns. On the trail of the last outlaw.

Previous to all this (off camera, so to speak) Johnny, who is now well into his thirties, has lured Rose to America, married her in California, cheated on her, and run away. He's got a hair trigger heart, although he's not a bad kid when he's sober. With Augie Blood on his trail he vows to redeem himself—go back to California and win back Rose's love and forgiveness. He's trying to get back home, to Rose, to Ireland, to the old songs . . . but he's forgotten where home and love is. He seeks redemption. Clawing at it.

In the midst of his Homeric flight he runs into a cousin, Joseph Dutton, who has been down and out on the streets of Laredo. Joseph Dutton is a Civil War veteran, fallen into a life of dissipation, but Joseph claims that he's now seen the light and aims to clean up his life. He'll quit the drinking and whoring and gambling and travel to Hawaii to devote the rest of his life to helping Father Damien in a leper colony on Molokai. The ultimate sacrifice. Joseph and Damien are based on historic characters of the same name.

Johnny becomes fixated with this strange story of Father Damien, who hails from Tremolo, Belgium, and has devoted his life to the outcasts of the world. Lepers. Johnny knows the spirit of Damien will watch over him, so Johnny prays to Damien each night. He considers following Dutton to Molokai, but first wants to see Rose.

Johnny continues his vow to redeem himself with Rose, turn his life around, and save his soul. Damien and Joseph Dutton are the ultimate cowboy figures for Johnny, because of their epic and wild spiritual journey across the frontier, to the end of the West—the Island of Molokai and a leper colony. The edge of the cowboy world.

Johnny is haunted by all this—and the voices he hears out beyond the campfire at night: Indian voices and chants, old cowboy songs, Mexican *corridos,* Swiss Yodel Choirs, French ballads . . . the bedrock of American music.

Part one ends with Johnny riding hard into Mexico, during the Revolution, and then up to Canada, Augie blood hot on the trail. Everywhere around him—campfires to saloons—he hears those songs and haunting voices. He's trying to follow them home.

❧ CURTAIN ON ACT ONE ❧

Synopsis Act Two:
Love is the last frontier

Yes, God I am angry
Yes, God, I am scared
Yes, God, I am lonely
Yes, God, this is my prayer
The road from anger to forgiveness
is a long and brutal journey . . .

—Rose Malloy, "I Talk to God"

"The Water is Wide" opens Act Two, signifying the gulf between men and women reaching for love. This side is devoted more to the woman's point of view. Johnny was in Mexico and Canada, on the run, and has finally ridden to California to beg forgiveness of Rose Malloy, whom he married years ago and jilted. Locked out of her small ranch, he sneaks in and climbs up to her bedroom window at night. She shoots him, thinking he's a bear.

Johnny, wounded, crawls off under a fence, and they embark on a twisted, late-night dialogue—she holds a gun to his head and tells him he needs to climb up "Resurrection Mountain."

Over the course of Act Two, Rose, in many voices, now sings up her version of the West in old songs which portray an abandoned woman's side: "The Railroad Boy," "Silver Dagger," "The Waggoner's Lad" (the last two edited out) and others. Meanwhile Johnny becomes a spiritual wanderer—looking for love and a path home. Lost. The Marshal is still on his trail. Singing those blood and guts hymns.

Augie Blood finally catches up with Johnny and arrests him for the old manslaughter charges, plus other trumped up transgressions, and Johnny is pistol-whipped and sent first to Angola Prison in Louisiana, then to Sugarland Prison Farm in Texas. He hears the songs and voices of the black prisoners: Lead Belly and Moses "Clear Rock" Platt singing old cowboy songs. Johnny is almost 60 years old now.

Johnny, the aged outlaw, is finally released in ten years and continues his spiritual wandering, eventually having a breakthrough moment in a bar in Tularosa that the long way around might be the shortest way home. The old West is mostly gone now. He's used it up. His meanness has left him. He believes Rose has moved back to Ireland, but all his letters were returned to him in prison, marked: "no such place." He's long forgotten that years ago he misspelled the town name. His memories come now in fragments. He wonders if Rose ever existed.

In the meantime, Marshal Augie Blood went to the bad, fell off the wagon, literally, and died a drunk by his own hand beneath the tree where Johnny was to be hung thirty years back. Joseph Dutton made his way to Molokai and helps Damien in the leper colony, and continues his work there long after Damien dies.

Johnny can't make Molokai. He'd rather keep it forever in his mind, as a spiritual idea, instead of a hard reality. He makes his way back east, singing in bars and pubs for tips, singing the old Irish songs and sharing cowboy tales. He makes enough to sail back home to Ireland. He follows his own trail back. Singing it up. The song lines.

Finally, he walks the same midnight road back to Roscrea and finds Rose in the old family house—she moved back to Ireland to tend the farm after her brother died. They become friends, or at least old folks looking out for each other, and Johnny is allowed to live above the stable in back. He builds a living space in the same loft where Rose's old man beat the "living shite" out of him almost seventy years ago. On Saturdays, he rides her old horse into town (for a pint) and the kids call him Old Cowboy John.

And so, full circle we've come. The road from anger to forgiveness has been a long and brutal journey out on the last frontier. Johnny and Rose have seen the West. They've sang the West, and they are home. Hearts mending. They drink to their time in the Wild West every Christmas.

> *Yes, the sea was wide, but we sailed o'er*
> *We rode the broncs, 'til they were broncs no more*
> *We were cowboy to the core*
> *Out on your last frontier*
> *And now love is the last frontier*
>   —"The Stable"

❧ CURTAIN ON ACT TWO ❧

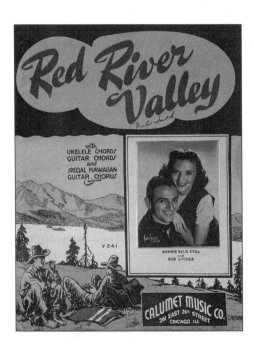

The Rose of Roscrae:
The Complete Lyrical Ballad
Act One

Oh, Bury me not, on the Lone Prairie
Where the coyotes howl, and the wind blows free
In a narrow grave just six by three,
Oh bury me not, on the lone prairie . . .

❧ OVERTURE ☙

Medley: **BURY ME NOT ON THE LONE PRAIRIE/**
THIS IS THE LAST FRONTIER/THE STREETS OF LAREDO/
RED RIVER VALLEY/HOME ON THE RANGE/
GOODBYE OLD PAINT/THIS IS THE LAST FRONTIER

* * *

I left my home in Templemore, County Tipperary, in the 1880s. Age 16. Torn away from my first love, the Rose of Roscrae. Sailed to America. A cowboy for to be! Like Sam Bass! I'd heard the songs and read the dime novels. Looking back now, from ninety years, at odd fragments. It started with a hangin' in the middle of the story, so to speak. Always towards redemption or oblivion . . . and a cowboy song! Out where love is the last frontier.

* * *

Love is the Last Frontier!
Love is the Last Frontier!

This is the Last Frontier!
This is the Last Frontier!

We got Cowboys, we got Indians,
We got Irish people too
We got Chinamen and Mexicans
They'll sing their songs for you

We came West to build a country,
Based on law and love and truth
This is the Last Frontier!
This is the Last Frontier!

We've hired gunslingers as Sheriff's,
Takes a crook to know a thief
And they who shall transgress,
Shall be hung up in a tree!

Irish Johnny Dutton is the worse of all of these!
This is the Last Frontier!

Love is the Last Frontier!
Love is the Last Frontier!

*   *   *

Guilty! Guilty! Guilty! Guilty!

JOHNNY BEHIND-THE-DEUCE (THE HANGING)

Judge: Mr. Johnny-Behind-the-Deuce, we find you guilty of murder, horse thievery, white slavery, card sharking, opium snortin', common drunkery . . . You, sir, are a range bum, a windmill monkey, curly wolf, whore-monger— you are olde Raw-head-and bloody-bones-himself !

Chorus: Guilty! Guilty! Guilty! Guilty!

Judge: What you got to say for your last words, Johnny?

Johnny: I never killed no one who didn't need killin'!

Judge: Those were John Wesley Hardin last words! Plagiarist!

Johnny: Don't let it end like this, tell them I said something!

Judge: Those were Pancho Villa's last words!

Johnny: How about . . .

> *What is life?*
> *It's the flash of a firefly in the night*
> *It's the breath of buffalo in the wintertime*
> *It's the little shadow which runs across the grass and loses itself in the sunset*

Judge: Those were Crowfoot's words, you forked-tongue bastard!

Johnny: Whatever.

> *Hangman, Hangman slack your rope*
> *Slack it for awhile.*
> *I think I see my sweetheart comin'*
> *Ridin' many a mile*

That's "Child Ballad Number 95," Judgie!

*   *   *

I'm Johnny Behind-the-Deuce
What is real? And what is truth?
It's all a dime store novel! Why the hell should I grovel?
I'm Johnny Behind-the-Deuce!

I'm Johnny Behind-the-Deuce
My head is in the noose
I'm about to die, why in hell would I lie?
Johnny Behind-the-Deuce!

Oh the West forever won
With a bottle, horse, and gun
Tombstone whores and cartel wars
Washed in whiskey, blood, and opium

Judge: Enough palaver . . . What do you want for your last meal, Johnny?

Johnny: Uh, Judge, I'll have a bone-in rib eye steak! Now I'll tell you exactly how I want it cooked . . . tell the hangman he can wait. I want an dry-aged slab of beef, one day above bein' rotten, blistered on a wood fired grill. Basted with sea-salt and mustard, Judgie, medium rare. You can send my congressman the bill. And a bottle of whiskey, Cuban cigars, and Mexican whores, maybe a little opium.

Judge: Forget it! Your last words first if you please.

Johnny:
When the green hills are covered with talking wires, and the wolves
*   no longer sing,*
What good will the money you paid for our land be, when no buffalo remain
*   to be seen?*

Judge: Those was Chief Seattle words, you slit-tongued Mockingbird. We are God Fearing pioneers, we shall not tolerate your godless rant, we have civilized this territory and you're the last outlaw heathen. Your last words, please, then the rope shall dance!

Johnny: A pioneer? That's a man who turned the grass upside down, then strung barbed wire over the dust that was left. Poisoned the water, cut down the trees and killed the Indian who owned the land, and called it Manifest Destiny and progress!

Judge: Those were Charles M. Russell's words, you lyin' snake. You forked tongue bastard!

Johnny:
Don't overplay your part, Judge,
Hand me that gun and let's vamoose
It's time for the great escape
Of Johnny Behind-the-Deuce.

Chorus: *Guilty!*

Johnny:
I slipped the noose, and someone slipped me a gun
I've stolen a horse, now I'm on the run
The judge was in on this, that corrupt old drunken clown
Go build a posse, friends, and try to run me down.

Murder, Corruption, Godlessness and lies
This country won't be civilized till Johnny dies
'Til they put a couple quarters my dead man's eyes
Make him me a carnival exhibit in the great by and by, ha ha!

I'm Johnny Behind-the-Deuce!
That's right, I slipped your noose
You bastards mettled now I got old scores to settle
Johnny Behind-the-Deuce!

Your West Forever won
With a bottle, a woman, and a gun
Trouble rides the fastest horse
Once again I'm on the run.

SAM HALL

Oh, my name it is Sam Hall it is Sam Hall
Oh my name it is Sam Hall it is Sam Hall
Oh my name it is Sam Hall and I hate you one and all
Yeah I hate you one and all, blast your eyes!

Oh I killed a man they said so they said
Oh I killed a man they said so they said
I killed a man they said and I bashed in his head
And I left him lyin' dead, goddamn his eyes!

And now in heaven I dwell yes I dwell
And now in heaven I dwell yes I dwell
And now in heaven I dwell, holy Christ, it is a cell
All the whores are down in hell, goddamn their eyes!

THE ROSE OF ROSCRAE

Come all ye homesick fools and drifters
The hour has come to sing the truth
There's a time for sober introspection
And a time to cut the wild dogs loose

Now I've got a roaming disposition
A wandering eye and a raging thirst
It's driven me to the furthest reaches
To escape first love and all the hurt

Now I can see a map of Ireland
In the dregs of bitters in this empty glass
And I can feel her breast against me
The Rose of Roscrae, wild Irish lass

Now I can feel her father's fists
As he knocked me 'cross that stable floor
And I left my blood and tears behind me
As I walked all night from Roscrae to Templemore

We sailed away and went half crazy
On the last frontier of your Western states
Haunted by hearts left behind us
Like the sweet young Rose of old Roscrae

There's nothin' for it, lads, but to sing the old songs
Carrickfergus to Ragland Road
So raise your wild harps, and lift your glasses
Sing up the lips we'll kiss no more.

HAIR TRIGGER HEART

Cowboys we are, and cowboys we shall always be.
  [José Doroteo Arango Arámbula (Pancho Villa)]
Don't let it end like this, tell them I said something . . .
  [Pancho Villa's last words]

They say trouble rides a fast horse, they say forgiveness rides a mule
Ah hell, they say a lot of things, that's why I have lived by my own rules
A man is seen in fragments—a scar, a limp, tattoos, and broken teeth
Scratch the surface on most men out here—you'll find two men hiding underneath

But I come not here to lecture to you of good and evil, black and white, right or wrong
I come to sing my story up—I'm the Black Jack Davy of those old gypsy songs
"A loose cannon," this they've called me—a half-cocked, cowboy Bonaparte
With my war bag full of cheap tricks, dead certain of my hair trigger heart

Oh Baby I got a hair trigger heart!

I've known love from every angle, I never learned the art of the graceful getaway
The poetry eludes me, I don't give a damn what the minor poets say
I'm not an alcoholic, I'm a drunk—there's a difference! Set 'em up Joe, make it smart!
I hail from horse traders and half breeds and a savage long line of
    hair trigger hearts

All the old gunfighters are leavin' town
Pistol packin' mama lay that pistol down
I'm still around—and I've got one more round
And I will hit the mark with my hair trigger heart

At the far end of eternity you might find me at a pub they call
    The Sodden Highwayman
I'll have a wax museum mustache—might be missing several fingers on my
    trigger hand
I'll have forgotten half the alphabet, my name and age, my Chinese laundry mark
But 'tween instinct and oblivion, mister, I will always hang on to this
    hair trigger heart

HE'LL BE DEAD BEFORE HE HITS THE GROUND

Deputy Joe Eagle: Friends, come gather round. We're lookin' for the man called Johnny Behind-the-Deuce. Son of an outlaw named Spanish Johnny, he travels with a greaser name of Cholo and a corrupt judge called Squig.

Marshal Augie Blood: This Johnny Behind-the-Deuce is also known as Joseph Dutton, Rotten John, and Dish Water Jake.

Deputy Joe Eagle: Boys I tell ya, you want a cowboy to eat a horse turd, put it inside a pie crust. If you want people to listen to a wanted man spiel, offer a reward and put it into a square dance.

Marshal Augie Blood: Swing your partner round and round, hang 'em by the neck and cut 'em down—he'll be dead before he hits the ground . . .

*　　*　　*

The Fiddling Fatman: Say fellas, if this here is a cabaret show, you gotta have a dance!

YOU GOTTA HAVE A DANCE

Now if this here was a Broadway show
We'd have to have a dance, ya know,
Square Dance, Line Dance, Cotton Eyed Joe,
And the Dance Hall Girl saloons

Irish Jigs, French Ballet,
Tap Dance, Tango, Jarabe!
German Polka, Flamenco ¡Olé!
Ballet Folklorico!

Paso Dobles to Navajo dancin'
Charros with their pony's prancin'
Western Swing for sweet romancin'
You gotta have a dance!

Now Augie Blood with his Gospel trains
Tracks me across the Texas Plains
I'll maybe dance on his remains,
'Cause you gotta have a dance!

Yeah I'm headin' for the Texas plains
Where as a kid I pulled on them bridle reins
Worked for Goodnight, there's a name!
Saw the last of the buffalo dance!

ST. JAMES HOSPITAL

Oh I been bull dodgin'
Ridin' way West, out on the plains
I was whoopin' up my cattle
I was ridin' the dailies
And I know I'm a poor cowboy
And I know I done wrong

Oh, bring me my pony
Let me up and ride on him
Then, oh, my dogies you got to be still
Oh the next high dry country
Will be your new quarters
Way out in West Texas
Up on some hill
Whoo-a-whoo-hoo . . . .

AIN'T NO MORE CANE ON THE BRAZOS

Ain't no more cane on the Brazos
    whoa whoa whoa
It's all been ground down to molasses
    whoa whoa whoa

You shoulda been on the river in 1910
    whoa whoa whoa
They were driving the women just like they drove the men
    whoa whoa whoa

Go down Old Hannah, don'cha rise no more
    whoa whoa whoa
Don't you rise up 'til Judgment Day's for sure
    whoa whoa whoa

Ain't no more cane on the Brazos
    whoa whoa whoa
It's all been ground down to molasses
    whoa whoa whoa

THE LAST RUNNING (FOR JOHN GRAVES)

Old Charlie Goodnight stood out on his porch on an isolated West-Texas ranch
Out in the yard were nine mounted ol' warriors—reservation Comanches
They were chattering in broken Spanish/Comanche and Charlie laughed at their
*   Indian cunning*
They wanted a buffalo from Charlie's private herd, they yearned for one last
*   buffalo running*

Old Iron Head, the leader, warbled-on about a time when the land and buffalo
*   was everyone's—meant to be shared*
Before the white man, the Iron Horse, and the barbed wire—so the Comanches
*   figured a gifted buffalo was fair*
Charlie kept fourteen head on a far hill, so he could gaze at 'em—as he drank
*   whiskey in the evenings*
Charlie's favorite was old Shakespeare, a horse killing bull,
*   but the beast had a spirit Charlie truly believed in*

Now back in the time of blood and confusion, the Comanches were the fiercest of
*   mounted tribes*
But smallpox, syphilis, and whiskey had scoured their numbers and eroded
*   their pride*
Now in beat-up old Stetsons and calico shirts they smoked and waited in the
*   shade of a Mesquite stand*
Finally Charlie relented and yelled, "All right, ye red bastards—take one for the
*   old days and civilization be damned!"*

Charlie turned to me and declared: "Dammit Kid, once was a world you won't
*   ever be knowin'*
The Comanche raids, the Staked Plains, the Bosque Redondo, the great trail
*   from Texas up to Wyoming*
The wild buffalo on a thousand hills, or a campfire song—one cowboy and his
*   guitar a strummin'*
Hang and rattle, boy, hold fast, and remember this well, the last of the buffalo runnin's"

Now Charlie gave Iron Head his choice from the herd, and of course the chief
*   picked Charlie's favorite, Shakespeare*
And as Charlie sat on the porch awaiting the run, we knew he was fighting back tears
A tear for the bull and the passage of time, an old life that would never come again
The Comanche, the buffalo, the vanishing West—just dust on the dry Texas wind

Our vaquero, Juan, tricked the bull into a chute, where old Shakespeare 'bout
*   tore the rails apart*
The warriors waited on broke down old ponies as Charlie waited with his
*   broke-up old heart*
The Juan turned the bull loose and it was all Comanche Blood Memory, wild
*   war whoops and arrows and shrieks*
Old Shakespeare fought like the king of the bison, one you could kill but
*   never defeat.*

The Indians cut up the meat and sang a buffalo song, a deep guttural sound—
   their ancient prayin'
And Iron Head rode up and saluted Charlie Goodnight as the Comanche rode
   off 'cross the West Texas plain
And me I was wonderin' did I see what I saw? The wild shrieks and the death of
   that bull?
It's stuck with me more than most things I've witnessed and all that history I
   ever learned in school

Yes, I's just a kid twelve years of age and the frontier was soon dyin' then done
But now that vision returns back through 70 years of reflection, my own the
   blood memory of that last great buffalo run.

*   *   *

(Coda: From Stephen Vincent Benet's "The Ballad of William Sycamore")

Now I lie in the heart of the fat, black soil,
Like the seed of the prairie-thistle;
It has washed my bones with honey and oil
And picked them clean as a whistle.

And my youth returns, like the rains of Spring,
And my sons, like the wild-geese flying;
And I lie and hear the meadowlarks sing
And have much content in my dying.

Go play with the towns you have built of blocks,
The towns where you would have bound me!
I sleep in my earth like a tired fox,
And my buffalo have found me.

HOME ON THE RANGE

Oh, give me a home, where the buffalo roam
Where the deer and the antelope play
Where seldom is heard a discouraging word
And the skies are not cloudy all day

Home, home on the range
Where the deer and the antelope play
Where seldom is heard a discouraging word
And the skies are not cloudy all day

How often at night, when the heavens are bright
With the light from the glittering stars
I've stood there amazed, and asked, as I gazed,
If their glory exceeds that of ours

*   *   *

Johnny: And out on the range one night I heard Walt Whitman, on an old wax cylinder, reciting his "America" poem:

AMERICA

America . . . . Centre of equal daughters, equal sons,
All, all alike endear'd, grown, ungrown, young or old,
Strong, ample, fair, enduring, capable, rich,
Perennial with the Earth, with Freedom, Law and Love

JUST A CLOSER WALK (WITH AUGIE BLOOD)

Just a closer walk with thee
Granted Jesus hear my plea
Daily walking close to thee
Let it be, dear Lord, Let it be

I am weak but though art strong
Jesus keep me from all wrong
I'll be satisfied as long
As I walk, let me walk, close to Thee!

Augie: My name is August Jeremiah Blood. My people come from Germany and other places I can't pronounce. I'm a Federal Marshal by job, a Baptist Preacher by inclination. My motto is "Capture 'em, convert 'em, or kill 'em." I'm a singin' sort of Preacher.

I travel in a covered wagon pulled by four mules: Mathew, Mark, Luke, and John. They's the Gospel Mules. Got me a little upright piano in the back of my wagon—I play old hymns as I ride through Indian Territory trackin' murderers and other scum.

I am washed in the blood of Jesus! I come into that Indian country armed with God, spiritual music, and guns. Got me a Smith and Wesson Scofield .45 pistol. Took it off Jesse James in a crap game. Got a Remington New Model Army .44, sturdy as hell, and a Peace Maker .45 with a snub nose.

In my left boot I carry a Smith and Wesson Pocket .32—you could cold-cock someone with it. The final word is a sawed-off, American Arms 12-gauge shotgun. Spits out a wide blast at a short range. You could take down five Greasers and a Chink, though I ain't prejudiced. All scum are equal in the eyes of God and Augie Blood.

❧ COWBOY VOICES BEYOND THE CAMPFIRE ❦

A. THE SKY ABOVE, THE MUD BELOW

Two men rode in from the south
On a rainy autumn night
The sky above, the mud below

They walked into the Deacon's bar
They were Mexican by sight
The sky above, the mud below

They threw a horsehair bridle down
"We trade this for whiskey rounds,"
The Deacon slammed a bottle down
The two men started drinkin'.

B. THE ROAD TO FAIRFAX COUNTY

Oh once I loved an outlaw, he came and stole my heart
Oh how I count the hours since we were torn apart
On the road to Fairfax County, I spied a highwayman
He wanted all my money, my heart beat like a drum
I gave him all my money, and sweet he smiled at me
His beauty I took pity, beneath the black oak tree

C. BLOOD ON THE SADDLE

There was blood on the saddle
And blood all around
And a great big puddle
Of blood on the ground

A cowboy lay in it
All bloody and red
'Cause a bronco fell on him
And mashed in his head

HE WASN'T A BAD KID, WHEN HE WAS SOBER

Midnight in Stinking Springs,
He disappeared like he had wings
His Ma said he was a decent kid, when he was younger

Mes'cans called him "Bilito"
Where do you come from Cotton Eyed Joe?
He swam the straight and narrow, then went under

Born in the brothel or born in the Bronx,
Born in the deep Missouri swamps
Like Jesse James or Curley Bill from Boulder
None of 'em were bad kid kids when they was sober

Dysfunctional, ill abused,
White trash, plum confused
He'd cheat at cards and tip the table over

He had anger issues, you understand,
At fourteen years he killed a man
But he wasn't a bad kid when he was sober

Racist, sexist, moved to Texas,
Passed a dozen worthless checks
Killed three men and beat it cross the border
Not a bad sorta human when he was sober

They went west to breath fresh,
Killed Indians and Grizzly bears
Cowboy life was dirty work done sober
The beef was tough, the pay was sad,

No wonder Mama's boy turned bad
With every snort of whiskey he grew bolder
Deep down he was a Christian-hearted soldier
Not a bad sort of kid when he was sober

Broke from jail, shot two down,
Sang as he rode out of town
He could sorta carry a tune when he was sober

Robbed from the rich, gave to the poor,
Or some old one-legged whore
He was Robin Hood, so sayeth the reporters

Build the legend when they die,
Like buzzards baked in apple pie
Create the Myth and then crust the details over
They were Christian-hearted kids, when they was sober

I'll tell you how The West was won,
By whiskey, guts, and hired guns
Chinese hop and coke and cartel soldiers

They loved to drink and bang the gong,
Pure opium from old Hong Kong
Some of 'em had monkey's on their shoulder

Make 'em heroes in the song,
Swap the right stuff with the wrong
Like narco-corridos *from the Mexican border*

Hired guns are the same this whole world over
Like Billy the Kid and Curley Bill from Boulder
None of 'em were bad kids when they was sober.

THE SIDEKICK'S LAST TESTAMENT

Judge: I've written this little note, Johnny. I'm gonna read it to 'ya here by the campfire:

I don't wanna be no more sidekick, Johnny
The "king of the punchline" type of guy
Out here sleepin' in the cold, with our boots on
I could be home drinking cognac, smokin' a pipe

When I was a judge I was at the top of the world
Lookin' down on the scum of the earth
The wicked and dumb were jailed, judged, and hung
Cursin' the day of their birth

I was corrupted by money and the chance for adventure
Irish whiskey and young Chinese girls
Here we are, on the run, with a posse behind us
Hidin' in holes like squirrels

I'm sick of bein' the butt of your jokes, Johnny,
Like Tonto, or Snuffy the Pimp
I got a decent mind and a law degree
I'm tired of this cowboy horseshit

So watch your back, Johnny, and show some respect
And judge lest ye not be judged
This sidekick might turn—your ass might get burned
Your bravado will down in your half breed blood

Sincerely,

Judge Squig

[The sound of gunfire. Judge buried in a shallow grave. With his boots on.]

JOHNNY'S CAMPFIRE SOLILOQUY #1

I'm Johnny Behind-the-Deuce,
Runnin' wild, and drunk and loose
The judge defected, I was disrespected,
One bullet and I cooked the bastard's goose

Augie Blood is on my trail,
He wants to toss my ass in jail
All the across the Indian territories
His old Prairie schooner with Cross on the sails
   and his upright piano in the back
   and his gospel mules
   and creepy songs about nailin' Jesus to a tree

Me I'm a drunken failed Irish Catholic kid with a lust for whiskey and whores!
What's the "Rock of Ages" got to do with me?
Behind every old cowboy song I got in my head there's a long Scots-Irish line
"Streets of Laredo," "The Unfortunate Rake,"
To "The Young Girl Cut Down in Her Prime"

It was on the streets of Laredo I met Joseph Dutton
A Civil War vet damaged by whores and drink
One day he cleans himself up
Says he's going to Molakai, Hawaii
Help some guy named Damien care for lepers who stink (Unclean!)

I couldn't get this Damien person out of my head
A priest who came all the way from Belgium
Now here was your true cowboy, eh?
Gone as far west as he could West to Molokai!
To help lepers, the descent of a holy man into hell!
There's your Outlaw!

*   *   *

Unclean! Unclean! Unclean!

THE UNFORTUNATE RAKE

As I was a walking down by the Lock Hospital,
As I was walking one morning of late,
Who did I spy but my own dear comrade,
Wrapp'd in flannel, so hard is his fate.

Had she but told me when she disordered me,
Had she but told me of it at the time,
I might have got salts and pills of white mercury,
But now I'm cut down in the height of my prime.

Get six jolly fellows to carry my coffin,
And six pretty maidens to bear up my pall,
And give to each of them bunches of roses,
That they may not smell me as they go along.

Over my coffin put handfuls of lavender,
Handfuls of lavender on every side,
Bunches of roses all over my coffin,
Saying there goes a young man cut down in his prime.

Muffle your drums, play your pipes merrily,
Play the death march as you go along.
And fire your guns right over my coffin,
There goes an unfortunate lad to his home.

THE STREETS OF LAREDO

As I walked out on the streets of Laredo.
As I walked out on Laredo one day,
I spied a poor cowboy wrapped in white linen,
Wrapped in white linen as cold as the clay

"I can see by your outfit that you are a cowboy"
These words he did say as I boldly walked by
"Come an' sit down beside me an' hear my sad story
"I'm shot in the breast an' I know I must die"

THE HANDS OF DAMIEN

Oh the seas will swell when the rivers weep
And the world is washed in doubt and sin
Hope and kindness will prevail
In the healing hands of Damien

When I reach out for a healing prayer
Lost for words to say, and then
I close my eyes and feel his touch
The gentle hands of Damien

He placed his hands deep in the wounds
The Blood of Christ ran red again
He consoled the wretched of the earth
The hands and heart of Damien

Alone and wandering though dark of night
Up against the rain and wind
He leads me toward the light of dawn
The guiding hand of Damien

* * *

Unclean! Unclean! Unclean!

JOHNNY'S CAMPFIRE SOLILOQUY #2

This is the last frontier!

I had an abiding love for Damien
And his lepers of Molakai
His cowboy hat and huge hands
And his willingness to die
His faith and love and spirit
Put a tear inside my eye
Truly this was the last frontier!

But I terrible missed my Ireland
And the Rose of Old Roscrae
You see she'd moved to Californy
And we'd been married fifteen years ago today
But that was long ago—I took to whores and drink
I threw it all away!

This is the last frontier!

So I need her blessing and forgiveness
To finally turn my life around
The outlaw, the heathen
The drunken cowboy clown
I'll find the Rose of Roscrae!
Unless this Augie Blood hunts me down

This is the last frontier!

I'll find the Rose of Roscrae
Then I'll have turned it all around
Maybe then join St. Damien
Maybe then back to Ireland bound
Cause I miss my home in Ireland
The songs, the sessions, the Holy Ground!

I am Lost on the last frontier!
This is the last frontier!

CARRICKFERGUS

I wish I was in Carrickfergus
If only for nights in Ballygran
I would swim over the deepest ocean
The deepest ocean to be by her side

But the sea is wide, and I can't swim over
And neither have I the wings to fly
If I could find me a handsome boatman
To ferry me over, my love and I

THE WATER IS WIDE

(Prelude: The Juice of the Barley/Irish Names)

Johnny: And from that day to this I have wandered alone, a jack of all trades and a master of none. The sky for me roof and the earth for me floor, I shall dance out me days drinkin' whiskey galore . . .

With the names of the old places and songs ringin' in my ears: "The Fields of Athenry," "The Green Hills of Kerry," "The Cliffs of Doneen," "Spancil Hill," "The Mountains of Mourne," "The Rocky Road to Dublin"

Yah Bastards!

And "Raglan Road" and "Carrickfergus," Mullingar, "The Rocks of Bawn," The Wicklow Hills, "The Bridge of Toome," Glackamara, "And The Craic Was 90 In The Isle of Mann"

Ye bastards!

The water is wide, I can't swim o'er
Nor do I have, the wings to fly
Build me a boat, that shall carry two
And both shall row, my love and I

There is a ship and she sails the sea
She's burdened deep, as deep can be
But not as deep as this love I'm in
I know not if, I sink or swim

Of love is gentle and love is kind
A cactus flower when first its new
But love grows old and it waxes cold
Then it fades away like the morning dew

The water is wide . . . .

THE FAIRGROUND PUGILIST

Friends, move in a little closer now—just a little closer. Bring the young ones, they're gonna wanna to see this. Step right up! (Don't crowd, pal.) It's an educational show, folks. For the entire family.

The sport of boxing has its origins in the forms of hand-to-hand combat derived from the ancient civilizations of Egypt, Greece, and Rome! Presenting here once of the fiercest bareknuckle pugilists in the spotted history of the Carnival: Spanish Johnny! He's also fought under the name of Irish John Dutton and other *noms de plume* of pugilistic lore. Step up!

Try your luck for just one dollar. Just a dollar, friends. Any man, woman, or beast in the crowd who thinks he can survive two rounds with Spanish Johnny wins a ten dollar gold piece . . . think of it! Oh yes!

The rest of you can witness the fight for just one thin dime. One thin dime gets you into the tent. It's all happening now, right here. Kiddies get inside for just a nickel. And they get a chance to see and pet "Teeny Tiny Tony, The World's Smallest Pony." How's that, kids? Just a nickel.

Spanish Johnny—He licked the Gaslight Champion, the man whose punches caused the gaslights to go out in Singapore! In the legends of Fistiana and Pugilism, in the Bareknuckle Bowery Bars, he's the legend! Just a dime.

Step up now! Just a dime. A dollar gets you ten on the fistic challenge . . . Step up now—two minutes—and don't forget "Teeny Tiny Tony! World's Smallest Pony!"

JOHNNY'S CAMPFIRE SOLILOQUY #3

I keep hearing those old cowboys songs
In the shadows late at night
Out beyond the campfire
Ghosts that sing 'til morning light

This is the last frontier!

❧ Campfire Ghosts/Cowboy Voices ❧

A. Sonora's Death Row

Me and the boy's we cinched up our saddles and rode to Sonora last night
Gun's hanging proud, daring out loud for any one looking to fight
Card cheats and rustlers would run for their holes when the boys from the old
*   "Broken O"*
Rode up and reined on the street that they named Sonora's death row

Mescal is free at Amanda's saloon for the boy's from the old "Broken O"
Saturday nights in the town of Sonora are the best in all Mexico
They've got guitars and trumpets and sweet senoritas who don't want to let you go
You'd never believe such a gay happy time on the street called Sonora's death row

B. The Man Who Rode The Mule Around The World

I'm the man who rode the mule around the world
I'm the man who rode the mule around the world
Rode in Noah's ark, I'm as happy as a lark
I'm the man who rode the mule around the world

C. The Old Desert Sands

Oh Carry me over them old Desert Sands with the yellow moon shinin' on high
Let me breathe the sweet air of a pure desert night
My fair old pony and I
Now ridin' and ropin' now that's what I love . . .

D. The Castration of the Strawberry Roan

I was hanging 'round town
In a house of ill fame
Laying up with a twister
And a hustlin' dames
When a hop-headed pimp
With his nose full of coke
Beat me out of the girl
And left me stone-broke

When a stranger walked in Said he, "Say, my lad
Are you any good riding horses that's bad?"
Said I, "You damn right, that's one thing I can do
I'm a second rate pimp, but a damn good buckaroo."

E. SOLILOQUY #4

And if it ain't those cowboy voices
I hear ghosts, wolves, and crows
And an Indian songs that chills me
It's a haunted West, you know

The Crow poet Henry Real Bird
In the rain and wind and snow
The night is the last frontier
Dead of night on the Last Frontier!

[Sounds of Crows, Wolves, and Henry Real Bird reciting the "Crow Door Song"]

CRAZY HORSE

Crazy Horse, we Hear what you say
One Earth, one Mother
One does not sell the Earth
The people walk upon
We are the land
How do we sell our Mother?
How do we sell the stars?
How do we sell the air?
Crazy Horse
We hear what you say

CUSTER'S LUCK

Now Crazy Horse said, "hey, it's a good day to die"
Then he mounted his pony and rode into the fight
He saw blood in the river, he saw blood on the ground
On the day Custer's luck finally ran out

Now they said that his luck was next to none
He said that the 7th could whip anyone
Well the rifle shots roared and the arrows rained down
On the day Custer's luck finally ran out

JOHNNY BEHIND-THE-DEUCE #2

I'm Johnny Behind-the-Deuce
What is real and what is truth?
Trouble behind me, trouble up ahead
Pass the rum and turn the wild dogs loose!

I'm riding hard for old Mexico
Then maybe Californ'io
Find the Rose of Roscrae, escape Augie Blood
In the second act I shall steal the show

Oh the West forever won
By Irish drunks, ex-slaves, and mounted Mexicans
Trouble rides the fastest horse
Once again I'm on the run

A silent prayer in the chapel of Guadalupe
Then it's back on the gunpowder trail
I'll find the Rose of Roscrae and escape Augie Blood,
He'll never trap my ass in his Gospel jail

Or maybe I'll go to Molokai and help Damien out
Or back to Ireland, singing the old Irish songs
I'm just a bumblin' old fool out here on the gunfighter trail
Haunted from midnight to dawn

SHE TALKS TO GOD

She locks the gate,
She leaves the world behind her
She sleeps out on the porch in summer,
Where the mountain lions can find her

She talks to God, she talks to trees and birds
And anything that listens
The ghost in Spanish Oak Trees
The ghost of lovers in her kitchen

They say St. Patrick
He drove the snakes right out of Ireland
But the Irish man she married
Had a rattlesnake inside him

He went on down the road
Oh all the women that he's had
She changed the lock on my front gate
Good God, it made him mad

She talks to God, she prays to his only Son
She sees His hand in every sunrise
When her daily work's begun
She'll believe in love with every dying breath
Now and at the hour of her death

Yes, God, she is angry
Yes, God, she is scared
Yes, God, she is lonely
Yes, God this is her prayer

The road from anger to forgiveness
Is a long and brutal journey
But she'll pray to find forgiveness
With all the love inside

She talks to God
She prays to His only Son
She sees His hand in every sunset
When her work is done
And she'll believe in love with every dying breath
Now and at the hour of her death
She talks to God.

ROCK OF AGES

Rock of Ages, cleft for me,
Let me hide myself in Thee
Let the water and the blood,
From Thy wounded side which flowed,
Be of sin the double cure,
Safe me from wrath and make me pure

Not the labor of my hands
Can fulfill Thy law's demands;
Could my zeal no respite know,
Could my tears forever flow,
All for sin could not atone;
Thou must save, and Thou alone.

Nothing in my hand I bring,
Simply to Thy cross I cling
Naked, come to Thee for dress
Helpless, look to Thee for grace
Foul, I to the fountain fly
Wash me, Saviour, or I die.

THE GUNPOWDER SUNSET/OVERTURE

❧ CURTAIN ON ACT ONE ❧

The Rose of Roscrae:
The Complete Lyrical Ballad
Act Two

THE WATER IS WIDE

The water is wide, I can't swim o'er
Nor do I have the wings to fly
Build me a boat that will carry two
And both shall row, my love and I

Oh, love is gentle, love is kind
The sweetest flower when first it's new
But love grows old and waxes cold
And fades away, like the morning dew

OVERTURE (ACT TWO)
"RED RIVER VALLEY," "THIS IS THE LAST FRONTIER"

Love is the Last Frontier!
Love is the Last Frontier!
Love is the Last Frontier!

I TALK TO GOD

I lock the gate,
I leave the world behind me
I sleep out on the porch in summer,
Where the mountain lions can find me

I talk to God, I talk to trees and birds
And anything that listens
The ghost in Spanish Oak Trees
The ghost of lovers in my kitchen

They say St. Patrick
He drove the snakes right out of Ireland
But the Irish man I married
Had a rattlesnake inside him

He went on down the road
Oh all the women that he's had
I changed the lock on my front gate
Good God, it made him mad

I talk to God, I pray to his only Son
I see His hand in every sunrise
When my daily work's begun
I believe in love with every dying breath
Now and at the hour of my death

Yes, God, I am angry
Yes, God, I am scared
Yes, God, I am lonely
Yes, God this is my prayer

The road from anger to forgiveness
Is a long and brutal journey
But I shall pray to find forgiveness
With all the love inside

I talk to God, I pray to His only Son
I see His hand in every sunset
When my work is done
And I'll believe in love with every dying breath
Now and at the hour of my death . . .

I talk to God.

THE BEAR

The bear he came at midnight,
Walkin' up the wall
I grabbed my 25/35
Outside in the hall

The bear was at my window,
I put the gun against his head
But the first shot didn't kill him
He fell down, crawled to the riverbed

He waited there in the high grass
To make his final stand
I called the dogs and took the lamp
Followed bear blood in the sand

Six feet out he came towards me
All claws and tongue and teeth
In smoke and thunder it all played out
He lay there at my feet

You people want to judge me?
You might sing another tune
If you woke up at midnight
With a bear inside your room

I'm tired of people tellin' me how to live -
I'm so tired of people tellin' me how to live
I'm tired of people tellin' me how to live
I'm tired of people tellin' me how to live!

*   *   *

Johnny: After she shot me, I crawled off under a barbed wire fence, and she held a gun at my head, and we had this strange sort of deranged Shakespearean dialogue.

I said: Remember when there's a mountain lion eatin' wild pigs down in the river near the barn?

She said: I remember you put wild pig's teeth in your own jaw with glue.

I said: Every tooth in my goddamn mouth is a pig's tooth. I used to break horses out here . . . hobbled 'em to a dead man with a war bridle on 'em.

She said: You're delirious—gut-shot. My father taught me you walked through the country and you followed fresh animal track. That's where the water will be.

I said: To ranch these days, you gotta bow down now to the federal government and college-bred environmental people.

She said: We had us a big diggin' machine out here and it hit a den of rattlesnakes. Come out the next day and the machine was covered with 500 rattlesnakes. You know drinkin' is the only thing that gets you through.

I said: Drinkin'? I remember Will James stayed out here for three weeks. Never come out of his room. Drinkin' whiskey. Every once and awhile he'd get up out of bed and draw bucking horses on the mirror with a bar of soap.

She said: The only way you're gonna reach true love and forgiveness, mister, is to climb up Resurrection Mountain.

THE RAILROAD BOY

She went upstairs to make her bed
And not one word to her mother said
Her mother she went upstairs too
Saying, "Daughter, oh daughter, what's troublin' you?"

"Oh mother, oh mother, I cannot tell
Its the railroad boy that I love so well
He courted me my life away
And now with me will no longer stay."

"There is a place in yonder town
Where my love goes and he sits him down
And he takes that strange girl on his knee
And he tells to her what he won't tell me"

RESURRECTION MOUNTAIN

Thunderstorms and cotton sheets
It's a long way from Resurrection Mountain
One day all souls shall meet
On the long road up Resurrection mountain

St. Augustine sang his lonely song
A long way from Resurrection Mountain
Down on his knees in the desert dawn
So far from Resurrection Mountain

Love love love
What's to become of me?
Love love love
Rain down and set me free

Lead me on up
Resurrection Mountain

We have lived our lives in solitude
A long way from Resurrection Mountain
But we pray with all our gratitude
One day we will climb Resurrection Mountain

They hammered nails into His flesh and bones
A long way from Resurrection Mountain
Then He rolled away . . . rolled away the stone
Rolled it on up Resurrection Mountain

And way out in the wilderness
St. Augustine does sings
And way high on the mountain
Resurrection rings, but it's a long way up
Resurrection Mountain

WHEN THE WOLVES NO LONGER SING

Oh the raven flies o'er these valleys, but he don't make a sound
O'er the deserts and the cities, he's refusing to look down
And the old songs are forgotten, gone with the Raven on the wing
And love not longer matters, and the wolves no longer sing

Now the old man sold his horses, and his children sold the ranch
And there's roads all through that valley, where his ponies used to dance
The dry wind sings a lonesome tune, a longing for the Spring
And love no longer matters, and the wolves no longer sing

The Old Man sold his Kingdom for a song
What's happened to the music? Where have the wild ones gone?

The rain will come again one day, the stars will keep on shinin'
And the poets will return again, magic melody and rhymin'
And if God is out there somewhere, looking down on everything
Then love will always matter, and the wolves will always sing

Then Love will always matter, and the wolves will always sing

THE GOSPEL OF JOHN, CHAPTER 4

At Jacob's well the woman said to Jesus, "Sir, give me this water, so that I may
not be thirsty or have to keep coming here to draw water."
Jesus said to her, "Go call your husband and come back."
The woman answered and said to him, "I do not have a husband."
Jesus answered her, "You are right in saying, 'I do not have a husband.' For you
have had five husbands, and the one you have now is not your husband. What
you have said is true."
The woman said to him, "Sir, I can see that you are a prophet!"
The woman left her water jar and went into the town and said to the people:
"Come see a man who told me everything I have done. Could he possibly be
the Messiah?"

JESUS MET THE WOMAN AT THE WELL

Jesus met the woman at the well
Jesus met the woman at the well
Jesus met the woman at the well
And He told her everything that she'd done

Well, He said, "Woman, where is your husband?"
Well, He said, "Woman, where is your husband?"
Well, He said, "Woman, where is your husband?"
She said, "Lord, I have none"

Well, He said, "Woman, you had five husbands"
Well, He said, "Woman, you had five husbands"
Well, He said, "Woman, you had five husbands"
But the one you have now is not yours"

Well, she went runnin' into the city
Well, she went runnin' into the city
Well, she went runnin' into the city
"The Man told me everything I'd done"

DAMIEN (A CRUST OF BREAD, A SLICE OF FISH, A CUP OF WATER)

Damien! I'm back out on the street again
Not homeless, but I need a friend
A friend who's been there too

Damien! I'm callin' out your name again
Did you ever close your eyes, back then?
Do you miss your childhood home?
(And Damien said)

I recall the smell of coffee roasting
On the childhood streets of Tremelo
And the biscuits made of ginger
Stacked like fairytales in bakers' windows

As I dreamed myself to Belgium
On stormy Tropic nights
As the ocean pounded Flemish songs
Upon the rocks of Molokai

I need no Red French wine
No tender lambs for slaughter
A crust of bread, a slice of fish, a cup of water

Damien! They're tearin' down your name again
But Robert Louis Stevenson
Shall defend your honor now

Damien! They'll burn you at the stake again
You who never did pretend
To be holier than thou

(Damien said) The quality of love and mercy
Is a chain around my soul that never breaks
Not even when my eyes grow cloudy,
And my crippled hands begin to ache

In this Mission life what must be done
Need not be said
I see only hope and life
On the Island of the Dead

I need no Red French wine
No tender lambs to slaughter
A crust of bread, a slice of fish, a cup of water

Damien! This is where I say "Amen!"
The story doesn't have an end
We journey on and on

Damien! Your prayers have kept me safe again
You who are my closest friend
I shall praise you in this song

There is a shrine in Bergen, Norway
For the man they say cured Leprosy
And I thought of you in Molokai
And how your children had finally been set free

And your church bell near the Leprosarium
Rang your name around the world
And Across all Kingdom Come

I raised a glass of Red French wine
Wrote these words for my dear brother
Who lived on love alone, a crust of bread, a cup of water!

GUADALUPE

There are ghosts out in the rain, tonight
High up in those ancient trees
And I have given up without a fight
Another blind fool on her knees

And all the Gods that I've abandoned
Begin to speak in simple tongue
Lord, suddenly I've come to know
There are no roads left to run

She is reaching out her arms tonight
Yes, my poverty is real
I pray roses shall rain down again
From Guadalupe on her hill

But who am I to doubt these mysteries
Cured in centuries of blood and candle smoke?
I am the least of all your children here
But I am most in need of hope

VALENTIN DE LA SIERRA

[rough English translation]

Voy a cantar un corrido
de un amigo de mi tierra,
llamabase Valentin
que fue fusilao' y colgao' en la sierra

No me quisiera acordar
era una tarde de invierno,
Cuando por su mala suerte
cayó Valentin en las manos del
    Gobierno

El Capitan le decia
cual es la gente que mandas
Son ochocientos soldados
que tienen sitiada la hacienda de
    Holanda . . . .

I am going to sing a ballad
Of a friend of my country
His name was Valentin
He was shot and wounded in the mountains

I would not like to remember
It was one winter afternoon,
When for his bad luck
Valentin fell into the hands of the
    Government

The Captain was saying to him
Which are the people that you ride with?
There are eight hundred soldiers
That have the ranch of Holland besieged

The colonel asks him
Which are the people that you guide?
There are eight hundred soldiers
That follow Mariano Mejias

Before coming to the hill
Valentin began to cry
"My mother of Guadalupe
For your religion they are going to kill me"

"Fly away, fly away little dove
Stop in the small fortress"
These are the early mornings prayers
Of a Brave man, who was Valentin!

POOR MOTHER MEXICO (OLD MERCADOS AND MARIACHI HORNS)

Poor Mother Mexico
So far from God, you know
Cerca de los Estados Unidos *and all those* la frontera *ghosts*
So far from the land where we born
Old mercados *and* mariachi *horns*

Poor mother Mexico
I am blinded by Sotol

Poor Mother Mexico
The land was once ours, you know
But they stole it away
They call us greasers and redskins
Some day we will win it back again
The land will be ours my friend—Ole! y Ole!

GALLO DEL CIELO

Carlos Zaragoza left his home in Casas Grandes *when the moon was full*
No money is his pocket, just a locket of his sister framed in gold
He headed for El Sueco, *stole a rooster named* Gallo del Cielo
The he crossed the Rio Grande with that rooster nestled deep beneath his arm

Gallo del Cielo was a rooster born in heaven so the legends say
His wings, they had been broken, he had one eye rollin' crazy in his head
He'd fought 100 fights and the legends say that one night near El Sueco
They fought Cielo *seven times and seven times he left brave roosters dead*

Hola, my Teresa, I am thinkin' of you now in San Antonio
I have 27 dollars and the good luck of your picture framed in gold
Tonight I'll put it all on the fighting spurs of Gallo del Cielo
Then I'll return to buy the land that Villa stole from father long ago

CAMPFIRE SOLILOQUY #1

Johnny: *Wounded like a three legged dog*
I fled back to Mexico and I talked to God
I rode with Pancho Villa, I sang the songs
And up to Canada—En Canadien errant!

I had me the wanderin' sign!
Doomed to wander the earth for all time
Singing my way back home.
I heard the yodel choirs of Fredericksburg
Chilled my bones

Spanish, French, Swiss, Navajo
Carved their music in the American Stone

*   *   *

SWISS YODEL CHOIR   Canton Bern, Switzerland

*   *   *

Un Canadien Errant

Un Canadien errant,
Banni des ses foyers,
Parcourait en pleurant
Des pays etrangers . . . .

[English Translation by Edith Fowke]

Once a Canadian lad,
Exiled from hearth and home,
Wandered, alone and sad,
Through alien lands unknown.

Down by a rushing stream,
Thoughtful and sad one day
He watched the water pass
And to it he did say:

"If you should reach my land,
My most unhappy land,
Please speak to all my friends
So they will understand.

"Tell them how much I wish
That I could be once more
In my beloved land
That I will see no more.

"My own beloved land
I'll not forget till death,
And I will speak of her
With my last dying breath."

He'll Be Dead Before He Hits The Ground #2

Joe Eagle: Friends, come gather round! We're lookin' for a man they call Johnny Behind-the-Deuce. He's Satan on a single fire saddle, he's got him a roaming disposition, is known to hang out with Spaniards, Mes'cans and half breed Indians. Mostly he's mounted and semi-drunk. He's fond of Gin Rickey's . . .

Augie Blood: He'll break into a cowboy song for no good reason—they're inside his skull.

Joe Eagle: he got a Chinese tattoo on his trigger hand. Some Chink words from the game "Mah Jong."

Voice From the Crowd: The law don't say nothin' about killin' a Chink, Sheriff . . . Judge Roy Bean said that!

Joe Eagle: He ain't no Chink!

Augie Blood: He's of Irish and half Indian descent, his conversation is rapid with frequent curses, he has a fondness for the bottle.

Joe Eagle: His Chinese laundry mark is B dash 7 dash 9.

Augie Blood: His muscles twitch at the base of his jaw when he's not talkin' . . . the top of his left ear is carved out.

Joe Eagle: As far as morals, he don't know dung from wild honey.

Joe and Augie: Swing your partner round and round, hang 'em high and cut 'em down—he'll be dead afore he hits the ground

[The sound of gunfire in the distance as church bells ring and Johnny is arrested.]

DOIN' HARD TIME IN TEXAS

I'm doin' hard time in Texas
Hard time in Texas, boys
I'm doin' hard time in Texas
For the crimes that I have done
Like stealin' horses and forgin' checks
Broke every law you might suspect,
Killed men who showed me no respect
Sweet Jesus—comin' home to you

I left my home at age fifteen, I was my Mama's only child
She cried: "It hurts to see you got your daddy's blood drunked-up and runnin' wild"
Mama, I was sick of workin' that feedlot job for just two dollars a day
So I jammed a shot of nitro into the feedlot safe and blew that door away!

Got thrown into Angola Prison one time, I tell you, boys, I was framed
But I met me Mr. Huddie Lead Belly
He sang me "When I Was a Cowboy out on the Western Plains,"
Huddie played him a big ole Stella 12-string guitar
I also met a killer named Moses "Clear Rock" Platt
He sang me "St. James Infirmary," boys, now what you think of that?

WHEN I WAS A COWBOY

When I was a cowboy
Out on the western plains
When I was a cowboy
Out on the western plains
I made a half a million
Pullin' on the bridle reins

Come a cow ki-yicky
Come a cow ki-yicky-yicky-yeah
Come a cow ki-yicky
Come a cow ki-yicky-yicky-yeah

Oh, the hardest battle
Was it ever on the western plains
Oh, the hardest battle
Was ever on the western plains
When me and a bunch of cowboys
Run into Jesse James

❦ WEST TEXAS MONTAGE ❦

A. OVERTURE WITH RED RIVER VALLEY

From this valley they say you are going
I shall miss your bright eyes and sweet smile
For they say you are taking the sunshine
That has brighten my pathway a while.

Come and sit by my side if you love me
Do not hasten to bid me adieu
Just remember the red river valley
And the cowboy who has loved you so

B. DESPERADOS WAITING FOR A TRAIN

I'd play the Red River Valley
And he'd sit out in the kitchen and cry
And run his fingers through seventy years of livin'
And wonder, "Lord, has ever' well I've drilled run dry?"
We were friends, me and this old man
Like desperados waitin' for a train

He's a drifter and a driller of oil wells
And an old school man of the world
He taught me how to drive his car when he's too drunk to
And he'd wink and give me money for the girls
And our lives were like some old western movie
Like desperados waitin' for a train

From the time that I could walk he'd take me with him
To a bar called the Green Frog Cafe
There were old men with beer guts and dominoes
Lying 'bout their lives while they'd played
And I was just a kid they all called his "Sidekick"
Like desperados waitin' for a train

Then one day I looked up and he's pushin' eighty
And there's brown tobacco stains all down his chin
To me he's one of the heroes of this country
So why's he all dressed up like them old men?
Drinkin' beer and playin' Moon and Forty-two
Like desperados waitin' for a train

The day before he died, I went to see him
I was grown and he was almost gone
We just closed our eyes and dreamed us up a kitchen
And sang another verse to that old song
"Come on, Jack, that son of a bitch is comin'"

C. OLD PAINT

I ride an old Paint and I lead an old Dan
I'm goin' to Montana for to throw the hoolihan
They feed in the coulees, they water in the draw
Their tails are all matted and their backs are all raw

Goodbye Old Paint
I'm a leavin' Cheyenne

Old Bill Jones had two daughters and a son
One went to Denver and the other went wrong
His wife she died in a pool room fight
Still he keeps singing from morning 'til night

When I die take my saddle from the wall
Put it on my pony, lead him out of his stall
Tie my bones on his back, turn our faces to the west
We'll ride the prairies that we love the best

OLD RATTLEBAG BLUES (SOLILOQUY #2)

I'm Johnny Behind-the-Deuce
I'm paroled they turned me loose
From Angola State to Sugarland Farm
I heard the black men sing the cowboy blues

And at night through those prison cell bars
I could hear the street women singin' old songs
"The Silver Dagger," "Railroad Boy," "The Waggoner's Lad"
'bout all the men that done them wrong

Am I bound to wander through all the eternities?
Don Quixote riding a bone spavined nag?
Homer and his Odyssey, guitar on his back
The Minstrel Boy called the Old Rattlebag!

When the singer becomes one with the song
He'll live forever if he keeps moving along
The last frontier goes on forever and ever
Bangin' that eternal gong!

I'm Johnny Behind-the-Deuce
I'll go to Molokai and learn the truth
Or maybe back to Templemore to start it all over
Though I'm gettin' a little long in the tooth

MIDNIGHT WINE (WHITE LIES AND COLD CHARDONNAY)

Pitch black ol' midnight
Can't see two feet in front of my face
No stars, out tonight, no moon
And no human race

A little red wine at dinner
Eased all my trouble in mind
But white wine at midnight
Has driven me over the line

Thank God for the vineyards
Near that wild Russian River, up there
Oh, the breeze off the ocean kissed these grapes
And its a very good year

It goes down so smoothly
The Oak and apple entwined
Think I'll pour me another
Fly away on this old Midnight wine

Lord can you tell me where love goes
When it slips away?
Leaving nothing behind
But white lies and cold chardonnay?

Here a toast to survival
To all those that love's left behind
In the bars and back alleys . . . and bedrooms
We're just partners in crime

But we stolen a moment of bliss
from this ol' Midnight wine

I'll sing the "Empty Bed Blues"
To the lonely old hoot of an owl
They say 'forgive and forget'
These are feelings my heart won't allow

Forgiveness needs aging
It's a vintage that will take it's own time
And I live by an hour glass that's filled
With the old Midnight wine

WHISKEY IN HIS BLOOD

He had whiskey in his blood when he died
He had whiskey in his blood when he died
Had an ounce of pure cocaine, and three monkeys on a chain
He had whiskey in his blood when he died

He used to preach the Gospel every day
But he fell off the wagon, sippin' one too many flagons
Yes, he used to preach the Gospel every day

He used to be a lawman with a gun
But he lost the county's blessing, forced too many false confessions
Yes, he used to be a lawman with a gun

His name was Augie Blood so they say
He sang the Rock of Ages puttin' framed men into cages
His name was Augie Blood so they say

TULAROSA

In the caves at dawn, when the singer's voice is raw and broken . . . the red wine is crusted on the glasses and eyes are closed in exhaustion . . . that's when the singer and the voice and the song find their moment . . . —Federico Garcia Lorca

We've come so far, to lose our way
We've talked too much, now we got nothing more to say
Down on our knees, but we've forgotten how to pray
Welcome to midnight, in a bar in Tularosa

Love is a pathless land, you journey on and on and on
I'm like an old racehorse, baby, I've been runnin' on the outside rail too long
Maybe the long way around is the shortest way home
Must be true, James Joyce said that . . . in a bar in Tularosa

Tularosa, you old ghost ya, I'm all alone, I'm so alone
I'll sing the old songs, deep in my blood and bone
Maybe the long way around
Is the shortest way home

So what's the plot, please tell me how the story ends.
People don't really die for love or truth
They just want to close their eyes and sing and pretend
You've read all the great works of literature
But you don't know a damn thing about love, my little friend

Pull up a stool, welcome to Happy Hour in Tularosa

❧ IRISH MEDLEY ❦

A. RAGLAN ROAD

On Raglan Road on an Autumn Day,
I saw her first and knew
That her dark hair would weave a snare
That I may one day rue

I saw the danger, yet I walked
Along the enchanted way
And I said let grief be a falling leaf
At the dawning of the day

B. THE LAKES OF PONTCHARTRAIN

I said my pretty Creole girl, me money here's no good
If it weren't for the alligators I'd sleep out in the wood
You're welcome here kind stranger, our house it's very plain
But we never turn a stranger out at the Lakes of Pontchartrain

THE STABLE

So I went home to Templemore
Walked to Roscrae, knocked on her cottage door
Yes, she'd moved back in 1944
She took over the family house when her brother died

Ya see we kinda made our amends
Not lovers, no, just old cuddle-bone friends
They say you can't go home again
But I tell ya, boys, that's a bloody lie

I sleep above her stable now
The very place where her old man knocked me down
I ride her old grey mare into Roscrae town
The kids yell, "Look! There goes old Cowboy John!"

Like Jesus in a stable born
Like Damien sailing back around the Horn
I went back to the place where my heart was torn
My heart is healing now

We both saw your wild West
We're snug now, in our Irish nest
You can throw our bones in an old sea chest
Go on! And send us out to sea

Yes the sea was wide, but we sailed o'er!
We rode the broncs, now they're broncs no more
Yes, we were cowboy to the core
Out on the last frontier

And Damien died, now he's a saint
Well some they is, and some they ain't
Some break horses, or sing, or paint
Yeah, it's all just a talk with God

ISN'T IT GRAND?

Look at the coffin, great golden handles
Isn't it grand boys to be bloody well dead?

Let's not have a sniffle, let's have a bloody good cry
And always remember the longer you live
The sooner you bloody well die

Look at the flowers, all bloody withered
Isn't it grand boys to be bloody well dead?

Look at the mourners, bloody great hypocrites!
Isn't it grand, boys, to be bloody well dead?

Look at the widow, bloody great female!
Isn't it grand boys to be bloody well dead?

Look at the preacher, all bloody sanctimonious!
Isn't it grand boys to be bloody well dead?

Twenty-five Cents

STAGE RADIO SCREEN

ISSUE No. 3

POPULAR
COWBOY SONGS

15c

THE MOST WONDERFUL COLLECTION EVER WRITTEN

OF RANCH AND RANGE

CASEY JONES
HOME ON THE RANGE
SAN ANTONIO
ABDUL ABULBUL AMIR
RED RIVER VALLEY
GET AWAY, OLD MAN
THE RIDING SONG
DOWN IN ARKANSAS
LONESOME ROAD
GIRL I LEFT BEHIND ME
WHOOPEE, TI-YI-YO
OLD MONTANA
STEAMBOAT BILL
MY TEXAS HOME
FLYING TRAPEZE

YELLOW ROSE OF TEXAS
LONESOME FOR HOME
COWBOY'S TRADE MARK
ONLY AS FAR AS THE GATE
THE EAST-BOUND TRAIN
FRANKIE AND JOHNNIE
A COWBOY VOCABULARY
LITTLE JOE, THE WRANGLER
MAKE ME A COWBOY AGAIN
SHE'LL BE COMIN' ROUND THE
 MOUNTAIN
I'VE GOT NO USE FOR WOMEN
WRECK OF OLD NINETY-SEVEN
MAY I SLEEP IN YOUR BARN
SEVEN LONG YEARS
THE OLD CHISHOLM TRAIL
RAGTIME COWBOY JOE

SHY ANN

Published and sold by
HOBO NEWS
44 WEST 17th STREET
NEW YORK CITY, N. Y.

PRINTED IN U. S. A.

Notes On The Songs

The songs the cowboys sang . . . are raw collops
slashed from the rump of Nature, and never mind
the gristle.

—John Lomax, 1910

Note from Tom: *Come gather round me, people . . .* It is not my belief that good songs need any further detail, footnotes, or background information in order for the listener to enjoy them. That being said, I have a folkloric interest in how certain songs, lyrics, stories, and melodies evolved, survived, prospered and are carried forward and sung. By *the folk*. Notes on the performers follow this section.

Growing up on folk music, cowboy songs, and Broadway musicals, I thought the blending of those forms a fine idea. And here ye have it. The only problem with the so-called "Frontier Musicals" of my youth (examples: *Annie Get Your Gun, Oklahoma,* etc.): the songs were great as Big Stage Broadway tunes, but the stories and lingo, dialogue, and characters were inauthentic, to say the least. Cowboys conjured up by Tin Pan Alley. I thought a musical with an edgy story and authentic cowboy songs might be a grand idea. I've thought about that for twenty years.

Folklore note: Traditional Cowboy and folk songs, as sung in saloons, pubs, whorehouses, horseback, on the range, around campfires, and in bunk houses may have varied from versions published since the early 1900s by The Lomax Family, Howard Thorp, Carl Sandburg and others (ditto in the UK by Cecil Sharp, A.L. Lloyd et al.).

Songs were cleaned up, combined, edited, and bowdlerized—which is to say that sometimes the editors and collectors removed material which was considered repetitive, improper, or offensive—so the published lyrics, in some instances, might have become weaker or less effective, but flowed consistent. John Lomax was not shy about even adding his own verses.

Here's an illuminating note from Lomax himself in the original manuscript of his 1910 version of *Cowboy Songs and Other Frontier Ballads:*

> As for the songs of this collection, I have violated the ethics of ballad gatherers,
> in a few instances, by putting together what seemed to be the best lines from
> different versions . . . others cannot be printed for general circulation.
>
> To paraphrase slightly what Sidney Lanier said of Walt Whitman's poetry,
> they are raw collops slashed from the rump of Nature, and never mind the
> gristle . . . some of the strong adjectives and nouns have to be softened . . . there
> is, however, a Homeric quality about the cowboy's profanity and vulgarity that
> pleases rather then repulses . . . he spoke out plainly the impulses of his heart.
> But as yet so-called polite society is not quite willing to hear.

For a dose of bawdy original versions of traditional cowboy songs, before they were cleaned up, you might try Guy Logsdon's book: *The Whorehouse Bells are Ringing,* or those early Oscar Brand "Bawdy" records—if you want your ears to ring sometime ask an old cowboy to recite "The Castration of the Strawberry Roan." I've included the first verse below (my brother recites it on the record), but that's tame.

As my old friend Katie Lee once stated (I'm paraphrasing her): "some folklorists would have us believe that a cowboy wouldn't say 'horseshit' if he had a mouth full of it."

Among the traditional recordings on this record, I collected versions on ranches, recording studios, in dressing rooms, over the phone via an old cassette recorder, off old 78 records, and on and on. In that way I felt like a modern day John Lomax, Howard Thorp, or Cecil Sharp—putting my ear to the ground and finding versions of the songs I loved, and the singers I truly believe in. Here, then, is a *raw collop* of your *Amerciana*.

I've provided whatever traditional song histories and anecdotes I could dig up, and keep concise. But I am not a folklorist *to the manor bred*. I am an *aficionado* of great singers and old songs, and a songwriter sometimes too.

Enjoy the ride.

* * *

❧ ACT ONE — THE MEN'S VIEW ☙

1a. Bury Me Not on the Lone Prairie

Sung by Jimmie Dale Gilmore, originally from Lubbock, Texas. It's also been called "The Cowboy's Lament" and "The Dying Cowboy" and is considered, by some, to be the most popular traditional cowboy song.

The ballad is an adaptation of a sea song called "The Sailor's Grave" or "The Ocean Burial," or "Burial at Sea," which began: "O bury me not in the deep, deep sea." "The Ocean Burial" was written by Edwin Hubbell Chapin, a Christian preacher from New York, published in 1839.

The melody and lyrics were collected and published in 1927 in Carl Sandburg's collection of folksongs: *American Songbag*. Sandburg called the book a "ragbag of stripes and streaks of color from nearly all ends of the earth . . . rich with the diversity of the United States." Amen, brother.

1b. The Overture to The Rose of Roscrae

The medley of Melodies: "Bury Me Not on the Lone Prairie," "This is the Last Frontier," "The Streets of Laredo," "Red River Valley," "Home on the Range," "Goodbye Old Paint," "This is the Last Frontier."

On a demo, I sang the traditional songs as a medley and added one of my theme songs, "This is the Last Frontier," into the mix. I sent the raw tape to Sweden, to Mats Hålling, the arranger whom we worked with on *Aztec Jazz*. Mats wrote the arrangements for the Norwegian Wind Ensemble, one of the oldest continuing orchestras in the world, and we recorded it live in March, 2014 in Halden, Norway.

I wanted something that would open like a John Ford movie or a Peckinpah film, conjuring up a wide angle shot of Monument Valley, and a lone rider, summoned up by those wonderful melodies we'll never get out of our heads.

2. This Is The Last Frontier

An opening theme which begins the opera. Sung by high school kids from The Waverley School of Pasadena.

3. Guilty/Johnny Behind-the-Deuce

We begin *in medias res*. In the middle. Our hero/villain/protagonist—is on the gallows making his last statement and his culinary wishes for his last meal, prompted by the corrupt Judge Squig, played by David Olney.

I meant it to have the tone a cross between Keith Richards and Warren Zevon (*Excitable Boy*). Raw guitar rock with Johnny ripping off famous quotes from Western history. John Wesley Hardin, Pancho Villa, Crowfoot, CM Russell, etc. Johnny is already in a fugue state, conjuring up history past, present, and future at odd angles. He's been hit in the head too many times during his forays as a Carnival Pugilist. He slips the noose and rides away with the corrupt judge as his sidekick.

4. Sam Hall

The quintessential hanging song, sung here by Johnny Cash, off his *Ballads of the True West*. Prior to the mid-19th century it was called "Jack Hall," after an English thief, who was hanged in 1707 at Tyburn. Jack Hall's parents sold him as a *climbing boy* (chimney sweep) for one guinea. Sir Percival Pott stated, "The fate of these people seems peculiarly hard . . . they are treated with great brutality . . . they are thrust up narrow and sometimes hot chimnies [sic] where they are bruised burned and almost suffocated." No wonder Jack Hall turned to crime.

5. The Rose of Roscrae

Roscrea lies in the center of Ireland and I've played many a concert there for a fine man named Tom Stapleton. Down the road, in Templemore, I have an 80-year-old aunt, Mary Russell, who lives in the family house. She raises cows.

I was trying to write an Irish drinking song and came up with the lyric and story, but didn't find a melody which suited it. I sent it to Gretchen Peters, and she and her husband Barry Walsh wrote the music. Bang! The melody worked perfectly and conjured the terrain.

I wasn't looking for this song to be the title piece, but when Maura O'Connell (*The Voice of Ireland!*) sang it, I perceived that it was big enough the carry the load. In the final verse I was thinking of Thomas Moore's "The Minstrel Boy," who raised his *wild harp* to his shoulder and heads off to the song wars.

6. Hair Trigger Heart

"Cowboys we are, cowboys we shall always be . . . " —Pancho Villa

A man is seen in fragments, as in descriptions of fugitives off old wanted posters. A scar, a limp, tattoos. Johnny rides away cursing the throng. He's Gyspy Davy and every rag-tag outlaw that ever rode a spavined horse. His only excuse for all the mayhem he's caused in love and life is his hair trigger heart, which can send him off in any direction at any moment. He's a *quadrazoid:* outlaw, lover, saint and minstrel boy.

The *"I ain't an alcoholic . . . "* line I got from Rosalie Sorrels, during a hungover breakfast at a train station hotel in Toronto.

7. He'll Be Dead Before He Hits The Ground

Marshal Augie Blood (Augie Meyers) and his deputy Joe Eagle (Joe Ely) rouse the crowd and form a posse to go after Johnny Behind-the-Deuce. Many of the descriptions of Johnny I collaged off of vintage wanted posters from the Old West. The posters would describe bad teeth, prison tattoos, Chinese laundry marks, the propensity to curse and drink, hair lips, bullet hole scars, and so on.

8a. You Gotta Have A Dance

In my mind this was always a Broadway Musical. You had to have dancing, and there was plenty of opportunity for it in a Western theme: Line Dance, Square Dance, Irish Jigs, Step Dancing, The Mexican Hat Dance, French Waltzes, Cajun Polkas, German-Mexican Polkas, Dance Hall Girl Can Cans, Hawaiian Hula, Argentine Tango and on and on—you gotta have a dance! Fats Kaplin leads it off. Barry Walsh plays the saloon piano.

8b. St. James Hospital

We could spend an entire book on this one song. I chose this rendition when I heard Moses "Clear Rock" Platt sing it on the *Black Texicans* record on Rounder. The recordings were collected by John Lomax in prisons. Thanks to folklorist Hal Cannon for turning me onto the record.

I loved the way Moses sang the line: "Way out in West Texas . . ." as he mashed together several old cowboy lyrics and set them inside St. James Hospital. (Read about Moses in the performer's section of this book.)

John and Alan Lomax, recorded this version in 1933 at the State Prison Farm in Sugarland, Texas. The early folk songs titled "St. James Hospital" or "St. James Infirmary" are songs that sprouted and evolved between the old English tune "The Unfortunate Rake," "The Young Girl Cut Down in Her Prime," "Bad Girl's Lament," "Lock Hospital," and the American cowboy song "Streets of Laredo." "Streets of Laredo" has many variations, including "Lee Therin's Barroom," which I've heard Hedy West sing.

The actual St. James Infirmary was in London—a religious foundation for the treatment of leprosy. There was also a St. James' Workhouse, built on Poland Street in London in 1728. It sounds to my ear that Moses "Clear Rock" Platt is mixing up lines and ideas from: "When I Was a Cowboy," "Get Along Little Dogie's," and "The Streets of Laredo." Off the cuff.

Those Texas and Louisiana prisoners had the propensity, song knowledge, and musical chops to sing spontaneous songs made up of lines from hundreds of other songs, so that versions changed and morphed every time someone like Lomax stuck a microphone near their faces.

The songs were used to accompany dull, hard work, and were almost chants that sound to me to be an early form of black cowboy "rap." Early cowboy music clearly owes a debt to the creativity and poetry of black cowboys and prisoners.

9. Ain't No More Cane on the Brazos

"Ain't No More Cane on this Brazos" is a traditional prison work song from Texas. Prisoners who were sentenced to hard labor were forced to cut sugar cane along the banks of the Brazos River, where many of the State's prison farms were located in the late nineteenth and early twentieth centuries.

The words *Brazos* came from the full Spanish name for the river: *Rio de los Brazos de Dios,* The River of the Arms of God. The headwaters begin in Black Water Draw, New Mexico and the river winds through Texas, down to the Gulf of Mexico.

Sung here by Jimmy LaFave and Gretchen Peters with Jerry Douglas on dobro. The Band also did a great version.

10a. The Last Running

I wrote this based on a short story by John Graves, which in turn, was loosely based on a supposed real life incident in West Texas. The legendary rancher Charles Goodnight was approached by a ragged band of Commanche who were begging for a buffalo to run *in the old way*, one last time.

Charlie Goodnight (1836 –1929) is sometimes known as the "Father of the Texas Panhandle." He lived 93 years, was a renowned cowman, and along with Oliver Loving, established the Goodnight-Loving Trail, which eventually spanned from Texas up to Wyoming. He and Loving first drove a herd of feral Texas Longhorns up the trail in 1866. Goodnight also invented the chuck wagon. From 1876 he raised cattle and kept a herd of Native Bison and the herd's bloodline survives to this day in Caprock Canyons State Park.

In his younger days Charlie smoked up to fifty cigars a day, and in his later days, age 91, he married a 26-year-old distant cousin named Corrine, who became pregnant with their child, but miscarried. His was a legendary life on the last frontier.

The great Texas essayist J. Frank Dobie, who knew Goodnight, is quoted in *Charles Goodnight: Father of the Texas Panhandle* as having said:

> I have met a lot of good men, several fine gentlemen, hordes of cunning climbers, plenty of loud-braying asses and plenty of dumb oxen, but I haven't lived long enough or traveled far enough to meet more than two or three men I'd call great. This is a word I will not bandy around. To me, Charles Goodnight was great-natured.

10b. The Ballad of William Sycamore

Between the years 1928 and 1943, Stephen Vincent Benét was one of the best-known living American poets. His books sold well and he was more widely read than Robert Frost and T.S. Eliot. "The Ballad of William Sycamore," published in the *New Republic* in 1922 and as a pamphlet in 1923, was a great success and a leap forward in his personal craft. This poem summons up a West of mythical proportions and is in rhymed verse.

Steve Young, an important American songwriter who was an early pioneer in what became known as *country rock,* and *outlaw music* (back when this was meaningful in the late 1960s) wrote music to many verses in Benet's poem and his version appears on several of his fine records. (www.steveyoung.net)

11a. Home on the Range

Dr. Brewster M. Higley (1823–1911) originally wrote the words in a poem called "My Western Home" in the early 1870s in Smith County, Kansas. The poem was first published in a December 1873 issue of the *Smith County Pioneer* under the title "Oh, Give Me a Home Where the Buffalo Roam."

The music was written by a friend of Higley, Daniel Kelley (1845–1905). Higley's original words are similar to those of the song today, but not identical. The song was adopted by settlers, cowboys, and the lyrics have been altered over the years.

John Lomax, in 1910, published a version which had a verse about Indians—"Oh the red man was pressed from this part of the West . . . " Lomax was known to combine different versions he'd heard, and even make up a verse when it suited him. It was, and is, called "the folk process."

It's the state song of Kansas.

11b. America

Born on May 31, 1819, Walt Whitman is the author of *Leaves of Grass* and, along with Emily Dickinson, is considered one of the architects of a uniquely American poetic voice. This is a shard from a wax cylinder recording.

> *Centre of equal daughters, equal sons,*
> *All, all alike endear'd, grown, ungrown, young or old,*
> *Strong, ample, fair, enduring, capable, rich,*
> *Perennial with the Earth, with Freedom, Law and Love,*
> *A grand, sane, towering, seated Mother,*
> *Chair'd in the adamant of Time.*

12. Just a Closer Walk With Thee

Taken from a Biblical passage from 2 Corinthians 5:7 which states, "We walk by faith, not by sight." It's a common song used in New Orleans jazz funerals. It dates back to southern African-American churches of the nineteenth century, prior to the Civil War, as some African American histories recall "slaves singing as they worked in the fields a song about walking by the Lord's side."

This version is sung by Augie Meyers (Marshal Augie Blood) as he rides through the West tracking down Irish Johnny Dutton. Augie tells us who he is and what kind of artillery he's packing.

13. The Sky Above, the Mud Below/On The Road to Fairfax County/ Blood on the Saddle

An outlaw medley from those haunting cowboy voices out beyond the campfire shadows:

Ramblin Jack Elliott sings a duet with me of my outlaw saga: "The Sky Above, the Mud Below," which I wrote about two twin Mexican horse thieves who hitch horsehair bridle stocks and quirts. I wrote the song after visiting a cowboy museum in Cochrane, Alberta, which had a beautiful pair of horsehair headstocks labeled: *braided by Mexican horse thieves, Montana State prison, 1910.* A lot of these anecdotes are in my book: *120 Songs of Tom Russell.*

"On the Road to Fairfax County" is a great contemporary outlaw song written by New York's David Massengill. The Roches did a fine version. David sings it here with the late Jack Hardy. Jack was a mainstay of the Village Folk scene from the '70s through recently.

"Blood on the Saddle" is the definitive, creepy Tex Ritter song. Tex had a voice that came at you like a Gila Monster crawling up your spine. The real deal.

14. He Wasn't a Bad Kid, When He Was Sober

I wrote this in Switzerland after I received a note from a rather well known Western artist—informing me that he had new information that Billy the Kid was a real hero of sorts. A true Irishman and a friend of the Mexican poor. The usual myths building up around legendary scumbags. I think he wanted me to write a song praising Billy. Sorry.

Billy was born in the Bronx and went downhill from there. He fought on the side of a rich English cattleman in the Lincoln County Wars, fought against an Irishman on the opposing side. The bastard! Just another hired gun—like a cartel warrior of modern times. The gun works for the highest bidder, his ancestry be damned.

15. The Sidekick's Last Testament

The corrupt Judge Squig, who has helped Johnny escape the noose, is fed up with life on the run. He was promised a lot of free whiskey and young Chines girls, which have not materialized. The judge delivers his speech—an eloquent letter terminating his position as Johnny's sidekick. The Judge is shot and buried in a shallow grave. With his boots on. David Olney is our performer.

16. Johnny's Campfire Soliloquy #1

Johnny fills us in on having to kill the sidekick, the corrupt Judge Squig, and then Johnny encounters Joseph Dutton on The Streets of Laredo. Dutton is on his way to Molokai to devote his life to helping Damien in the Leper Colony.

In medieval times—*Unclean!*—was a warning lepers were required to shout out whenever they approached someone on the road—warning people to stay clear. The lepers also carried a cow bell they rang.

17. The Unfortunate Rake/The Streets of Laredo

Our cowboy story winds from the border town of Laredo, Texas all the way back, almost 300 years, to a syphilis hospital in London. A trail of tears. Variants and tributaries of the cowboy song "Streets of Laredo" snake through: "The Cowboy's Lament," "St. James Infirmary Blues," "St. James Hospital," "The Young Girl Cut Down in Her Prime," "The Bad Girl," "The Unfortunate Lad," "The Unfortunate Rake," "One Morning in May," "The Whores of the City," "Lee Therin's Barroom," and probably a dozen or two more.

The melody is similar to the Irish song "The Spanish Ladies." The story: someone is dying in the gutter because of syphilis or a gunshot or a knife blade. Soldiers, sailors, maidens and cowboys—cut down in their prime and lamenting on their lives. Can you imagine this storyline being so durable in the folk canon? Hell yes.

We arrive back at Lock Hospital, which opened in London on 31 January 1747. Lock was the first venereal and infectious disease clinic and the most famous and first of the Lock Hospitals. There was also a Lock Hospital in Dublin. Treatment for syphilis, back then, might include white mercury chloride salts, and even arsenic. There is mention of mercury powders in the early songs.

As far as bawdy verses, Austin and Alta Fife, Utah Folklorists, mentioned one source of the song who stated: "there were originally seventy stanzas, sixty-nine of which had to be whistled."

The Lock Hospitals turned to the treatment of syphilis as leprosy declined. Which leads us right into the next song of St. Damien and the lepers of Molokai.

St. Damien of Molokai   Joseph Dutton

18. The Hands of Damien

I noticed his hands first. His left hand was stretched down over his priest's cassock, a hand seemingly huge, but probably swollen, due to the effects of leprosy. His face was bloated with the disease, and he wore what looked to be a priestly cowboy hat. The photo was taken in the late 1880s in Molokai, Hawaii. He had but a few months to live.

I saw the photo in 2009 when St. Damien was canonized by The Catholic Church. It was the newspaper picture that struck me. Who was this guy? What was his journey? Belgium to Hawaii? The wild West! I read a few of the books—the main one being *Damien the Leper*, written by Mia Farrow's father, film director John Farrow.

Damien was born Joseph de Veuster in 1840, in Tremelo, Belgium— and died April 15, 1889, in Molokai Hawaii. A Belgian priest who devoted his life to missionary work among the Hawaiian lepers.

He was a difficult character, at times, and demanded what he thought was needed for the lepers of Molokai. He had his enemies in the Church, but was defended, in a long essay and pamphlet by Robert Louis Stevenson.

In the Farrow book I came across mention of one Joseph Dutton (April 27, 1843– March 26, 1931) a Civil War Veteran, cowboy, and drunk who cleaned up his life, joined a monastery and then traveled to Molokai and devoted the remainder of his life to Damien and the leper colony.

Brother Joseph Dutton worked on behalf of the lepers long after Damien died. He didn't wish to become a priest and he wanted no recognition for his sacrifices. My fascination with these two figures had nothing to do with the Catholic Church. I thought of their incredible spiritual journey—out on our last frontier.

What's this have to do with our cowboy story? Joseph Dutton, in our story, was the distant cousin to Johnny Dutton, our main character, and Joseph tells his own story on The Streets of Laredo. He crawls out of the gutter and is going to Molokai to work with lepers and Damien.

Johnny Dutton is so mystified and moved by Joseph Dutton's story that he holds Damien in his heart forever and vows to clean up his life -he talks and prays to Damien when the chips are down. It's a hard road.

In Johnny's mind these two historic spiritual figures: Damien and Joseph Dutton, are real cowboy heroes who have gone to the end of The West (Hawaii and Molokai) to devote their life to a higher cause and help the wretched of the earth. The outcasts.

They are the *Living embodiments of the Word*. Their journey seems impossible, but Johnny Dutton aspires towards that sort of goodness.

19. Johnny's Soliloquy #2—Campfire Revelations

Johnny sings of his fascination for St. Damien, his own yearning for Ireland, and his guilt at losing The Rose of Roscrae. He reveals that 15 years back he'd married her but ruined it all, cause he ran off and *took to whorin'*, but he's going to win her back . . . he'll gain her forgiveness. It's a long, brutal journey. You crawl up the trail to Resurrection Mountain on your knees.

20a. Carrickfergus

Sung here by the great Irish singer, Finbar Furey. "Carrickfergus" is one of the more beloved traditional Irish songs. One rumor is it that it's popularity owes to actor Peter O'Toole singing it to songwriter Dominic Behan in the 1960s (brother of Brendan Behan) and then Dominic Behan wrote the middle verse. *Perhaps*. Dominic Behan also wrote "The Patriot Game," the melody of which influenced Bob Dylan's "With God on Our Side."

"Carrickfergus" (from the Irish *Carraig Fhearghais*, meaning "rock of Fergus") is a town in Country Antrim, Northern Ireland. The song is a 19th-century translation of an Irish-language song (*"Do Bhí Bean Uasal"*). It also shares common lines with the old English folk song, from the 1600s, "The Water is Wide."

20b. The Water is Wide/The Irish Soliloquy

"The Water Is Wide" (also called "O Waly, Waly") is of English origin, dating to the 1600s. The English folklorist Cecil Sharp published the song in *Folk Songs From Somerset* (1906). It's related to Child Ballad 204, and shares a line or two with the Irish song "Carrickfergus": "the sea is wide, I can't swim over." This is a crucial line to Johnny Behind-the-Deuce, because he fears he'll never make it back home.

Johnny begins his soliloquy quoting from the old Irish song: "The Juice of the Barley," then name checks all the beautiful Irish place names from old songs, before he slides into singing "The Water is Wide."

Fairground Pugilist Booth, UK

21. The Fairground Pugilist

A carny spiel performed by Sourdough Slim. Irish Johnny Dutton is on the run and making a little road money working as a Carny pugilist. Taking on all comers. I wrote this loosely based around sideshow spiels I've heard over the years.

Fairground boxing was popular for two hundred years in England and Ireland, and many great British and Irish boxing hopes came out of the carnival circuit. In the early days it was all bareknuckle. In 1977 Muhammad Ali displayed his skills for charity in front of Ron Taylor's Boxing Emporium in the U.K.

Johnny Dutton gets his brain scrambled in the boxing booths and thus he develops four different personalities—he's a *quadrazoid*. Saint, sinner, minstrel, cowboy, what have you. It enables him to sing songs and duets with himself from many angles. He sees his life in fragments and song lyrics. He's trying to put the puzzle back together.

22. Johnny's Campfire Soliloquy #3

Johnny keeps hearing those outlaw voices, old cowboy songs, and Indian chants—out beyond the campfire in the haunted West.

23a. Campfire Ghosts/Cowboy Voices: Sonora's Death Row/The Man Who Rode the Mule Around the World/Old Desert Sands/The Castration of the Strawberry Roan

At times, late in the night, Irish Johnny Dutton hears voices singing out beyond the campfire. Sometimes he's singing to himself, but doesn't know it.

I chose this odd assortment for the poetry in the songs, but also the hard truth in these singer's voices. Blackie Farrell wrote "Sonora's Death Row," a song that has influenced some of my own songwriting. The turn of the screw plot. He sings it here in a dressing room in Reno several years ago. I first heard it by Leo Kottke. There is fine poetry here.

Muleteer and cowboy poet Ross Knox sings "I'm the Man Who Rode the Mule Around the World," which dates back to an old Charlie Poole record from 1925. It's a traditional boasting song related to "I Was Born About Ten Thousand Years Ago."

The cowboy-folklorist Glen Orhlin sang me "Old Desert Sands" in a dressing room in Elko, Nevada. Glen was about 80 at the time. He's had many albums out and several fine book collections of cowboy songs, including *The Hellbound Train*.

My brother, Pat Russell, recites the first verse to "The Castration of the Strawberry Roan," which is attributed to Curley Fletcher, the man who wrote the original "Strawberry Roan." You can look up the rest yourself. Bloody and obscene as hell. Gives you an idea what the boys recited around the bunkhouse. Brother Pat was listening to cowboy music, and singing it and reciting the poetry when he was 15, after he ran off into the High Sierras of California to pack mules. He's cowboy to the core.

23b. Campfire Soliloquy #4

Johnny's hearing the haunting sounds of crows, wolves and Indian chants in his dreams and nightmares. Out beyond the campfire. Henry Real Bird, the Crow poet, is singing "The Door Song." He sang it to me over the phone from a cafe in South Dakota.

After he sang it, Henry stated:

> That was a doorway song. You sing it at the door of a teepee. I sang it the other morning in a celebration . . . haven't sang it in 30 years . . . I was horseback and sang it. I called the people awake before the rise of the sun. I was telling them to wakeup for a big day. Yeah, that's a doorway song.

Henry grew up ranching on the Crow Reservation in Montana, near the Custer Battleground.

24a. Crazy Horse

One does not sell the earth that people walk upon
We are the land? How do we sell our mother?
How do we sell the stars? How do we sell the air? . . .
Possession, a war that doesn't end . . .

This is the opening track to John Trudell's record *Bone Days*, produced by Angelina Jolie. "One does not sell the earth upon which the people walk," is a direct quote from Crazy Horse. John goes on to fashion a powerful poetic statement.

John is half Santee Sioux and one of the strongest performers I've had the pleasure to work with. I opened for John and his band in Italy a few years ago. I say more about John's life in the *Notes on Performer's* section. I think any record dealing with the West should be privileged to include such strong Native voices like John Trudell and Henry Real Bird.

24b. Custer's Luck

A portion of a song about Custer, and his last stand, written and sung by Thad Beckman, who has played guitar with me for several years. Thad is working on a record on The West. He's one of America's finest guitarists.

25. Johnny Behind-the-Deuce #2

Johnny on the run—on the way to Mexico, maybe Molokai, and finally to the Rose of Roscrae—seeking forgiveness, redemption, or extinction.

26. She Talks to God

I wrote the female version of this (in Part Two)—"I Talk to God"—based on many years of recording and filming my sister-in-law, Claudia Russell, and her history in the West. She grew up on a 30,000 acre old Spanish ranch, rich and deep with history—horse thieves, Indians, buckaroos, and all of it. I believe her family goes back eight generations in the Cuyama Valley. Then she ran into my cowboy brother Pat, a notorious cowboy in his own right. The lines "I lock the gate, I leave the world behind me . . ." come from Claudia. Also some of the dialogue in Act Two. She does not mince words. More about her up ahead.

27. Rock of Ages

"Rock of Ages" was written in 1763 by the Reverend Augustus Montague Toplady a preacher in Blagdon, England. Toplady, so it is told, was caught in a storm in the Mendip Hills and sought refuge in a rock formation in the gorge of Burrington Combe. He took out a deck of cards from his pocket and wrote the lyrics down on several of them.

When the ship SS London went down in the Bay of Biscay in January 11, 1866 the last man who left the ship could hear the passengers singing "Rock of Ages," so in that sense it rivals "Nearer My God to Thee" as a song sung on sinking ships.

This side rolls out with the "Gunpowder Sunset" overture performed by the Norwegian Wind Ensemble.

*   *   *

❧ ACT TWO — THE WOMEN'S VIEW ☙

1. The Water is Wide/The Overture

See previous notes on "The Water is Wide."

2. I Talk to God

My sister in law, Claudia, ranched alone for many years on a three thousand acre spread in the historic Cuyama Valley. She now has the help of her son, Jubel, and his family. I based this around her life—loosely. Claudia used to sleep out on the porch in summer and mountain lions would come very close to drink out of a pool. Hers is an epic and important life in the West. This is Rose's anthem. She lays her feelings on the line to God. Anger, fear, loneliness . . . the journey.

3. The Bear

Again—I wrote this based on real life stories told to me by my sister-in-law, Claudia Russell, who has been forced to shoot two bears inside her ranch house in California. (No she didn't shoot my brother.) Again, much of the woman's side to this story is gleaned from years of hearing Claudia's life story and family history.

The dialogue at the end of the song is loosely pieced together by fragments from Claudia, Pat Russell, and Jubel Russell. Yes, my brother used to glue wild pig's teeth into his jaw. It saved on dentist bills, and the nearest dentist was usually 100 miles away.

In our story Johnny gets his due for trying to sneak into Rose's house in the dead of night. She mistakes him for a bear. Shoots him. He crawls off under a fence, where they proceed to have this "Shakespearean" dialogue. No reconciliation here.

4. The Railroad Boy

"The Railroad Boy" or "The Butcher's Boy" is an American traditional folksong which traces back to English broadside ballads: "Sheffield Park," "The Squire's Daughter," "A Brisk Young Soldier," "A Brisk Young Sailor" and "Sweet William (The Sailor Boy)."

The story usually involves a jilted girl killing herself for love and leaving a final note requesting a deep grave, a marble stone, and a "white snow dove" or a "turtle dove" placed on her breast. In Scripture, a pair of doves was offered in sacrifice by Mary at her purification. (Luke 2:24) The pigeon and the turtle-dove were the only birds permitted to be offered in sacrifice.

In old folk songs doves are similar to roses and briars for signifying mourning, love, loss and sacrifice. Mexican *corridos* (see "Valentine de la Sierra" above) often end with the line *"vuela, vuela, palomita"*—"fly away little dove," etc., and send this message.

I've heard fine renditions of "The Railroad Boy" by Joan Baez, Tommy Makem, and Bob Dylan with Joan Baez. I used to sing it with my daughter, Quinn. Eliza Gilkyson seems to sing as if these songs came out of her blood and bones. Indeed, they do, since her father was a great composer of folk songs.

5. Resurrection Mountain

A gospel song I wrote after listening to Van Morrison's "And it Stoned Me" off of his *Moondance* record. Something about water and resurrection. There's a mountain near our El Paso hacienda called *Mount Cristo Rey,* where once a year the penitents crawl on their knees up to the statue of Christ.

Here, inside our story, Johnny Dutton needs to redeem himself. *Somehow.* The McCrary sisters, from Nashville, lend the proper gospel soul to this. They once sang backup for Bob Dylan in his gospel years.

Chief Seattle

6. When the Wolves No Longer Sing

When the green hills are covered with talking wires and the wolves no longer sing, what good will the money you paid for our land be then?—Chief Seattle

Chief Seattle was from the *Duwamish* tribe in the Northwest. I co-wrote this song with the great Ian Tyson who has been a major influence on my work. A song that speaks of the changing country, the dying West, the death of mystery and song, and a prayer that the wild things and the music will return. The master songwriter Gretchen Peters sings this.

7. The Gospel of John/Jesus Met the Woman at the Well

Come see a man who told me everything I have done. Could he possibly be the Messiah?
John 4 (16-29)

Marshal Augie Blood recites from the Gospel of John, Chapter 4. Which is the basis of the old gospel song: "Jesus Met the Woman at the Well." I sing it here with Eliza Gilkyson and based it on the early Ian and Sylvia version. Gurf Morlix tears it up on 12 string guitar.

Rev. Gary Davis, Dave Van Ronk, and Peter, Paul & Mary also did versions. For a kick ass, get down, authentic gospel take, check out the Mahalia Jackson live version. The real deal.

The song is a relative to the Child Ballads "The Maid and the Palmer" or "The Well Below The Valley." "The Maid and the Palmer" is a particularly gruesome saga of a maid at a well approached by a pilgrim (in the same manner that Jesus approaches the woman at the well) and the pilgrim asks for a cup to drink. She says she doesn't have a cup. He tells her to call her lover. She denies having a lover, and he tells her she's had lovers aplenty, and even illegitimate kids (maybe through incest) and this pilgrim in fact knows where they're buried. Grim indeed. The Jesus story is a little more upbeat.

9. Damien (A Crust of Bread, A Slice of Fish, A Cup of Water)

I wrote this in 2009. Worked on it a long time after I read *Damien the Leper*, by John Farrow after I'd seen a photo of St. Damien in a newspaper, after he was made a saint. Something there struck a deep chord, and it may be easy to say it harkens back to being raised a Catholic in my early years, but there's more than that. I was earlier drawn to the story of Our Lady of Guadalupe, but she was an apparition, or a vision, not a historical figure like Damien.

I then believed Damien belonged in this story—he lived in a far *Western* place, The Island of Molokai, and he wore this peculiar looking priest's hat that resembles a cowboy hat. He's a hero of mine. (For more see: "The Hands of Damien" above in Act One.) He lived in solidarity with the outcasts of the world.

It's a cowboy thing.

10a. Guadalupe

I wrote and recorded this on my record: *Blood and Candle Smoke,* and Gretchen Peters and I included her version on our Western record: *One to the Heart, One to the Head.* It's become my favorite song of the ones I've written. It's based on a moving experience I had sitting in the shrine of Our Lady of Guadalupe in Mexico City. The song has nothing to do with *religion,* it has to do with spirit and the faith of Mexican people devoted to *Our Lady of the Americas—the Mystical Rose.*

Valentine de La Sierra

10b. Valentine de La Sierra

I first heard "Valentine de la Sierra" on a jukebox in the Kentucky Club in Juarez, Mexico. Ana Gabriel was the singer. She tore through the heart of the song as I imbibed the three hand made margaritas. You see, the margarita was invented in Juarez. I'll never forget this voice.

"Valentine de la Sierra" is a popular *corrido* from the Mexican Revolution. Many versions exist. Valentín Avila Ramírez was a *Cristero* from Huejuquilla el Alto, Jalisco, who fell into the hands of the *agraristas* in the nearby region of Valparaíso, Zacatecas. He was interrogated regarding the movements of the *Cristero* forces, and was later executed by the federal troops. The true story is evidently complex, as it's difficult to figure out what side Valentine was really working for. Was he a spy? And for who?

Nevertheless I urge you to investigate Ana Gabriel's versions on You Tube. This is a song I always ask the Mariachi's for. In our story, Johnny Dutton is in Mexico, running from the law and soaking up the music.

Corridos relate to the old ballads. Many ballads were written and sold as single sheet broadsides. If someone was about to be hung in the public square, there might be an old one legged guy in the crowd selling a broadsheet ballad about the condemned man and his evil deeds, ending with an admonition to all good people to avoid the perils of a sinful life.

With all that in mind, consider the work of the Mexican José Guadalupe Posada (1852–1913) who was a Mexican political printmaker whose work has lasted a century, because of its satirical acuteness. He created broadsides—one page woodcuts with stories, corridos, songs, and tragedies cloaked in macabre Mexican humor, utilizing *calaveras*, skulls and skeleton figures made popular by the Day of the Dead ceremonies in Mexico. No tongue-in-cheek here. This is the insolent tongue bitten off, dropping into the gutter.

Lets bring back broadsides. Throw our newspapers and televisions away.

11. Poor Mother Mexico (Old Mercados & Mariachi Horns)

Poor Mexico, so far from God
And so close to the United States!
    —*Attributed to* Porfirio Diaz (President of Mexico, late 1800s)

I made this up on the spot, recording with accordionist Joel Guzman in Texas. I always loved this quote, which was attributed to the controversial seven-term President of Mexico, Pofirio Diaz—though his biographers deny he said it. I don't really know what it means, but it rings with certain poetry. I can almost see Juarez from my studio window. The quote could certainly relate to the recent drug war. 10,000 people died in Juarez alone.

In our story Johnny Dutton is banging around Mexico, on the run from the law. Music is everywhere. If this is an *Americana* record (a much mis-used term) then all forms of *North American* music should be referenced—Mexico up to Canada. Patagonia to the Yukon.

12. Gallo del Cielo

"Gallo" is one of the first songs I wrote (1978) and I devote a chapter to it in my book *120 Songs of Tom Russell*. It's a cockfighting *corrido* in English. It's had quite a history. Joe Ely does a fine version and I use a verse of it here sung by Ian Tyson, merely because I wanted Ian on this record. He single-handedly resurrected Cowboy Music back in the 1980s. He's been a big influence on my writing and singing.

13a. Soliloquy #1

Is Johnny doomed to wander the earth forever? He speaks of the music he encounters along the way, music which forms the bedrock of American Folk music—Mexican music, French Canadian melodies, German polkas, old cowboy songs . . . and he speaks of a Swiss Yodel Choir in Central Texas. The Swiss and German immigrants settled in different parts of Texas. At one time there was even a language called *Texas German*.

13b. Swiss Yodel Choir (on Swiss Independence Day)

I'm married to a Swiss psychologist and we spend part of our time in Switzerland in a little farm village. Outside my studio window I see Emmental cows, work horses, and horse carriages going by. The bakery opens at 6 a.m. and the local Inn is three hundred years old with a deep, ancient wine cellar.

Swiss Independence Day is celebrated August 1. The date is inspired by the date of the Federal Charter of 1291, when three Alpine cantons swore the oath of confederation. On Independence day in our little village there's a bonfire on the mountain and much singing from a Swiss Yodel choir, doing traditional songs which raise the hair up off your neck. I joined in this year, and sang, behind their backs.

So what's this have to do with our Wild West opera? A group of German-speaking Swiss settled the community of Schoenau, between Shelby and Industry, in Austin County, Texas in the late 1800s. They built a hall nearby and organized a singing society, *Helvetia Schönau Männerchor*, in the 1880s.

Fredericksburg, Texas was founded by Germans in 1846 and named after Prince Frederick of Prussia. The town is also notable as the home of *Texas German*, a cross between English and German. Mexican *conjunto* music, also known as *conjunto tejano*, was born out of south Texas at the end of the 19th century, after German and Swiss settlers introduced the button accordion.

So, you see, I wanted to throw in an authentic reference to real, old time Swiss music for the flavor. *Conjunto* music is huge today on the border, bringing us the *corridos* and *narco-corridos* full of the stories of historic and modern day outlaws.

14. En Canadiene Errant

I first heard Bonnie Dobson's name mentioned by young Bob Dylan on a radio show in the early 1960s. Bonnie is a Canadian who was a fixture in the '60s folk movement around Greenwich Village. She has since moved to London, England and has come to my shows there at The Cecil Sharp Center. It's an honor to know her. She's still singing and recording and sounds great. She allowed me to use her version of this song.

"*Un Canadien Errant* (A Wandering Canadian)" was written in 1842 by Antoine Gerin-Lajoie after the Lower Canada Rebellion of 1837–38. Some of the rebels were condemned to death, others forced into exile to the United States. The Acadian version is known as "Un Acadien Errant." Many Acadians migrated to Spanish colonial Luisiana, now Louisiana, where they developed what became known as Cajun culture.

15. He'll Be Dead Before He Hits the Ground #2

Joe Eagle and Marshal Augie Blood are moving in on Johnny. Soon there'll be a shoot-out and Johnny will be captured and sent to prison. Much of their spiel here is taken from old "Wanted Man" posters . . . *a man is seen in fragments.*

16. Doin' Hard Time in Texas

My Texas friend Jim Maxfield told me he woke up one night and dreamed up a song called "Doin' Hard Time in Texas." When he relayed the subject matter (rape, incest, murder, prison, redemption etc.) I told him it might be a bit much for me—it was a whole opera in itself—but I liked the title. So I refigured it for the story here. It also helps me get Johnny into Angola Prison and then Sugarland Farm in Texas where he can hear Lead Belly and also Moses "Clear Rock" Platt sing their songs, as recorded by John and Alan Lomax.

17. When I Was a Cowboy (Western Cowboy)

Composed and sung here, in prison, by the great by Lead Belly. This was Lead Belly's cowboy-blues riff on the West—in which he fights at Bunker Hill, and also runs into Jesse James and Buffalo Bill out on *the Range of the Buffalo.*

In 1930 Lead Belly was in Angola Prison Farm for an attempted homicide, charged with knifing a white man in a fight. It was one of his many times in prison. Earlier he had served time in Texas for killing a relative of his, over a woman. This version was recorded when Lead Belly was "discovered" in 1933 during a visit by folklorist John Lomax and his then 18-year-old son Alan.

The Lomax's recorded Lead Belly on portable aluminum disc recording equipment for the Library of Congress. Lead Belly was later released, following a sung petition the Lomax's had taken to Louisiana Governor Oscar Allen. It was on the other side of a recording of his signature song "Goodnight Irene."

Tom with Guy Clark in 2014

18a. West Texas Montage/Deperados Waiting for a Train

It was an overcast winter morning in February, 2014. I went for a visit with Guy Clark at his house on the edge of Nashville. Guy had just had two knees replaced. He'd been ailing for awhile, and we sat in his kitchen, looked out over the suburbs, and chatted. He was moving slowly, sipping coffee and hand-rolling cigarettes. The master songwriter.

Guy kept peering out the window, above the winter trees, like an old hawk with his furled brow—and I asked him if he missed West Texas. I thought maybe he was dreaming across a thousand miles to Monahans, Texas, where he was born.

"Hell yes," Guy said, "I miss it. I should have left this shit hole long ago."

I'd been listening to his songs back in El Paso, as I painted, and was thinking more and more of what a great songwriter he was and how he was able to summon up that wild patch of America—West Texas. Dozens of his songs gave me the chills. They don't make writers like this anymore.

At some point I asked if he was up for singing me a verse of "Desperados Waiting for a Train" for this project and he agreed to, and took me over, slowly, to a corner that had some of the guitars he'd made. There were also several paintings he was working on, and the portrait of Guy painted by his late wife Susanna. It was a moving experience—trust me. A house of memories. The house of an artist.

He slowly picked up the guitar and forced himself to concentrate, and then laid a verse down. Apologizing for a guitar flub he said, "I'll start over." I told him *no,* it was perfect. And it was. He was singing it as if he were back in Monahans in the 1940s. You can hear that.

Later in the studio the great Dan Penn came in and finished singing the song. Two master songwriters and a classic song about West Texas. Here's your soul music. Here's your *Americana.*

18b. Goodbye Old Paint

Old Paint had a colt down on the Rio Grande,
And the colt couldn't pace, and they named it Cheyenne . . .
    —Jess Morris

Carl Sandburg sang this song, and John Lomax collected a version for the Library of Congress, sung with fiddle, by Jess Morris at Dalhart, Texas, 1942. Dalhart is up in the Panhandle. Morris claimed to be the composer of the song (meaning the music), but later claimed he first heard it from an ex-slave named Charley Willis. Said Morris:

> After the Civil War in 1865, father hired an ex-slave by the name of Charley
> Willis—colored—who was about 17 yrs. old, to break horses for him. Charley
> was born in Milam County, Texas, an adjoining County. Charley had gone up
> the trail to Wyoming with the Snyder brothers, having driven their first herd to
> Wyoming in 1867. The Snyder's drove ten herds, consisting of about 1,500 head
> in each herd, and it was with one of those herds that Charley took the trail, and
> on one of those trips, Charley learned to sing 'Ol' Paint.'
>
> Charley played a jews-harp, and taught me to play it. It was on this jewsharp
> that I learned to play 'Ol' Paint,' at the age of seven.

So we must give African American Charley Willis a bunch of credit for this
song. And Lord knows where he heard it. Maybe he wrote it. Black cowboys made a
significant contribution to cowboy song history.

The song has been recorded by everyone with a love for cowboy music, from Carl
Sandburg to Woody Guthrie, Johnny Cash, Pete Seeger, Ian Tyson, and Linda
Ronstadt. Gretchen Peters did a fine version on a record we did: *One to the Heart,
One to the Head*. The melody was also utilized by Aaron Copland in his ballet, *Billy
the Kid*. Copland is considered one of the godfathers of Americana.

19. Old Rattlebag Blues (Soliloquy #2)

Johnny is released from prison. He's an old man, looking back. Inside the prison walls
he met Lead Belly and Moses "Clear Rock" Platt, and hears them sing their cowboy
songs. He's heard the women singing their laments out on the street. He's bound off
for Molokai, or maybe he'll sing his way back to the Olde Sod, Ireland. Singing old
songs in the bars. Busking. A Rake's Progress. Aching for The Rose of Roscrae. Don
Quixote on a bone-spavined nag, with his wild harp slung over his back, instead of
a gun. He becomes the old Minstrel Boy they call "Old Rattlebag."

20. Midnight Wine (White Lies and Cold Chardonnay)

Blame Ian Tyson for turning me on to good Chardonnay.

My favorite vintages come from the Russian River area up there on the coast of
Northern California. Something to do with vineyards and the ocean air. (Lord, please
send me a case of Chalk Hill or Rombauer).

I wrote this for the opera: our hero is turning to drink for solace. *A toast to
survivors* and all that. Forgiveness needs *aging . . . like a vintage that must take
it's own time . . .* I don't know if any of the last frontier cowboys soaked up any oak
barrel-aged Chard. But what the hell.

"*I drink to make other people interesting.*"—George Jones

21. Whiskey in His Blood

I had to kill off Augie Blood. He went to the drink, lost his mind, and shot himself
beneath the very tree where Johnny was to be hung—miles back in our story. Too
many blood and guts gospel songs destroyed his equilibrium. He wasn't a bad man,
when he was sober. His gospel mules ended up at Knott's Berry Farm, pulling kids
around in a wagon. His deputy, the half-breed Joe Eagle, disappeared into the desert,
and went *native*.

22. Tularosa

Our hero is at the end of the trail in a bar in Tularosa, New Mexico, where he attempts to cast a strong eye back on his journey. He concludes that *love is a pathless land*, and he's been *running on the outside rail too long*, but *maybe the long way around is the shortest way home*. I believe James Joyce said that one time . . . in Trieste or Tularosa.

Next stop: Templemore, Ireland.

23a. Irish Medley—On Raglan Road/The Lakes of Pontchartrain

"On Raglan Road" was fashioned from a poem written by Irish poet Patrick Kavanagh, named after Raglan Road in Ballsbridge, Dublin. It was first published as a poem in 1946 under the title "Dark Haired Miriam Ran Away," about Kavanagh's girlfriend Hilda. (Name changed to protect the innocent.) The relationship didn't last. Hilda was much younger than Kavanagh, and she went on to become a medical doctor and marry the Irish Minister of Health.

The poem was set to the music of the traditional song "The Dawning of the Day." An Irish-language song with this name (*"Fáinne Geal an Lae"*) was published by Edward Walsh (1805–1850) in 1847 in Irish Popular Songs, and later translated into English as "The Dawning of the Day." I recommend versions by Luke Kelly and The Dubliners, as well as Van Morrison and the Chieftains.

"The Lakes of Pontchartrain" is actually an American ballad about a man who is given shelter by a beautiful Louisiana Creole woman. Because, in my opinion, the definitive version is done by the Irish singer Paul Brady (with a fine guitar accompaniment) I've always considered it Irish. Lake Pontchartrain forms the northern boundary of New Orleans.

The liner notes accompanying Planxty's version state that the tune was probably brought back by soldiers fighting for the British or French armies in Louisiana and Canada in the War of 1812. Up for debate. As someone said in a recent folk debate: *folk music is not an exact science*.

There's an unusual cowboy version called "On The Lake of The Poncho Plains" in Margret Larkin's 1931 book, *Singing Cowboy, A Book of Western Songs*. Ms. Reva Cordell collected it from an unnamed cowboy at a rodeo in the late 1920s.

The bottom line is I love the line about the alligators out in the woods, and the description of the Creole' girl's hair *falling in jet black ringlets* on her shoulders. And in the end, the lovesick hero retreats to his local Inn where he raises *a flowing glass* to the Creole girl.

23b. The Stable

"The Stable" brings the story full circle. Our old cowboy-outlaw, Johnny Dutton, finally returns to Ireland, sings his way back home, by busking on the street and in bars, singing up the Old Ireland of his youth. He arrives and walks the ten mile road between Templemore and Roscrae. He knocks upon Rose's door. She's returned to Ireland and manages the family house in Roscrae. They have laid their swords and *wild harps* down. Peace.

They're friends now, or at least old folks who take care of each other. He sleeps in a room above her stable, the very place where her father beat the *holy shite* out of him almost 70 years back. He's the local Irish cowboy legend as he rides her old horse into town.

(I have an 85 year old aunt Mary Russell living in Templemore, so this one's for her.)

24. Isn't It Grand?

I heard the Clancy Brothers perform sing this in a big old Irish concert bar on Cape Cod back in the 1980s. There they were, the lads! Aran sweaters, pints in hand, they took the stage and began with: "Isn't it grand, boys to be bloody well dead?" There you have the best funeral song every sung. Their heads were cocked high and they sang the living hell out of it.

Various sources attribute the song to an English Music Hall performer named Leslie Sarony (1897–1985), who sang a song titled: "Ain't It Grand to Be Blooming Well Dead . . ." Leslie may have scribed some of these lyrics:

> *Lately there's nothing but trouble, grief and strife*
> *There's not much attraction about this bloomin' life*
> *Last night I dreamt I was bloomin' well dead*
> *As I went to the funeral, I bloomin' well said:*
>
> *Look at the flowers, bloomin' great orchids*
> *Ain't it grand, to be bloomin' well dead!*
> *Look at the florists countin' their profits*
> *Ain't it grand to be bloomin' well dead!*
>
> *Look at the lawyers readin' the will out*
> *Ain't it grand to be bloomin' well dead!*
> *Look at their top 'ats, polished with Guinness*
> *Ain't it grand, to be bloomin' well dead!*
>
> *Look at the earthworms bloomin' well wrigglin'!*
> *Ain't it grand to be bloomin' well dead!*

Leslie Sarony also wrote one titled "Why Build a Wall Round a Graveyard, When Nobody's Trying to Get In?" You gotta love this guy, and the English Music Hall tradition. I would love to sing "Isn't It Grand?" at somebody's funeral, the kind of deal where everyone is being sanctimonious, dry-weeping, folks that didn't give a shit when the old bastard or bastard-ess was alive, and are now trying to get at the money.

Isn't it Grand!

25. The Rose of Roscrae

And here we are, folks, back where we started. Walking the road from Roscrae to Templemore, right into the heart of Ireland.

And who better to sing it up then Maura O'Connell? After she'd nailed this in the studio, Maura turned to me and stated:

> Ah, but Tom you've missed two things: you've misspelled 'Roscrea' and, Tom, it's not really that far a walk from Roscrea to Templemore . . .

I answered:

> Maura, the lad's just had the holy shite beaten out of him. His mind is in fragments. It's a long journey, indeed, and spelling is the last thing on his jangled mind.

And there we'll leave you. Out on that road, in the dead of an Irish night. Seeking love and redemption.

Sláinte!

—Tom Russell 2014

The Performers
(in order of appearance)

❧ ACT ONE ❦

JIMMIE DALE GILMORE *as* **Old Rattlebag The Cowboy Minstrel** (vocals, guitar: "Overture," "Home On The Range," "Streets of Laredo," "West Texas Montage/Red River Valley")
www.jimmiegilmore.com

One of America's purest, *lonesome-est,* sounding country & folk singers. The high King of West Texas soul. Jimmie sings to the heart of cowboy songs. He's got West Texas in his craw. Jimmie Dale was born in Amarillo, Texas and raised in Lubbock. His father sang honky tonk music and Jimmie's first influence was Hank Williams. You can hear that, still, in his voice.

In 1972, Jimmie formed The Flatlanders with fellow Lubbockers Joe Ely and Butch Hancock. They recorded an American classic (*More of a Legend Than a Band*) later re-issued by Rounder. He's gone on to record dozens of great folk and country records and appear in films such as *The Great Lebowski.*

The Norwegian Wind Ensemble

One of the world´s oldest continuously running orchestras of any kind. A piece of Norwegian national heritage and part of music history. Based in Halden, Norway.

They've performed and recorded Early Music, jazz, classical, folk, blues, and rock. Some of their last recordings were of Frank Zappa material, an interpretation of Miles Davis' *Sketches of Spain*, and a collaboration with myself on my live record *Aztec Jazz*. This is a 32-piece wind orchestra which includes clarinets, saxophones, French horns, trumpets, trombones, bassoons, oboes, flutes, bass, and percussion.

For this project I sang a medley of cowboy material onto a tape and sent it to the Swedish arranger and composer Mats Hålling, who then wrote the charts for the overture. The piece was performed and recorded live at a sound check in Halden, Norway in March, 2014.

I was introduced to the orchestra by my longtime friend, writer Tom Skjeklesaether.

TOM RUSSELL *as* **Irish Johnny Dutton, Johnny Behind-the-Deuce, and other outlaw aliases and cowboy ghosts** (guitar, vocals, all field recordings)
www.tomrussell.com

I descend from Iowa horse traders. I was born in Los Angeles into a musical family. My uncle George played "The Star Spangled Banner" at Martin Luther King's March on Washington. My brother Pat rode bulls and sang cowboy songs. I took his Tijuana guitar and decided I'd love to be a songwriter when I heard Bob Dylan sing "Desolation Row" at the Hollywood

Bowl. I was later fortunate to write cowboy-based songs with one of my early idols, Ian Tyson. Ramblin' Jack Elliott and Ian were best men at my wedding in Elko.

The rest of the story is pretty much in the 30 or so records I've recorded and in the books: *120 Songs of Tom Russell* and *Blue Horse/Red Desert: the Art of Tom Russell*. The introductions to these books have a lot of early life stories, like meeting Bob Dylan and the Beatles. And the story goes on; I've been working on this cowboy-opera concept for 20 years, and it came to life a few years ago.

The Last Frontier Opening Chorus

Gretchen Peters, Barry Walsh, and Tom Russell joined by thirty students from the Waverley School of Pasadena, California, who were visiting Nashville and taking a tour of the recording facility. We threw them into the ballgame and they sang the chorus, giving us a great swath of real Western voices singing the opening, rather then professionals. Here's the street rabble demanding a hanging! All their names are listed on the CD packaging.

DAVID OLNEY *as* Judge Squig

(vocals, "Guilty/Johnny Behind-the-Deuce," "The Sidekick's Last Testament")

www.davidolney.com

David Olney deserves an Academy Award for his portrayal of the corrupt Judge Squig, sidekick to Johnny.

David is a top level American songwriter and covers the *noir domain* better than anyone. His writing and singing voice is right out of a Raymond Chandler crime novel, and his songs have been recorded by Johnny Cash, Emmy Lou Harris and a host of others. He's a riveting performer and I hear he's recently playing Hamlet in a road tour. Or was it Iago? All his albums are worth checking out at his website.

JOHNNY CASH

(vocals, "Sam Hall")

This traditional song comes from Johnny's: *Ballads of the True West* Album. A classic. I don't think I need to detail any of Johnny Cash's incredible career and his gift to American folk and country music. It's all on the records. When I was about ten years old my brother had the first Johnny Cash record: *The Hot and Blue Guitars of Johnny Cash*. Once you've heard that voice you don't forget it. It cuts through all the bullshit of day to day life.

Fast forward to the early 1990s and a breakfast I had with Johnny in Switzerland where we talked songs. Later he recorded a song of mine, "Veteran's Day." His *True West* recordings and his Native American tribute (*Bitter Tears—The Songs of Peter La Farge)* are bedrock American folk music. He did his research and he sang it up. He knew the West.

JOE ELY *as* **Deputy Joe Eagle**
(vocals: "He'll Be Dead Before He Hits The Ground" #1 and #2,
"Gallo del Cielo")
www.ely.com

Joe was born in Amarillo, Texas, and grew up in Lubbock. As
a teenager he ran off with the Ringling Brothers circus and worked
as a wrangler and looked after the world's smallest pony. He later
wrote about it all in his song "Indian Cowboy."

Joe formed *The Flatlanders* with fellow Lubbock souls Jimmie Dale Gilmore and
Butch Hancock, and later pursued a solo career which goes on successfully to this
day. He's performed with everyone from The Clash, Bruce Springsteen, The Rolling
Stones, Merle Haggard, and on and on. His original songs span the boundaries of
American music from folk to Tex Mex, soul, rock, to blues, and back. He can rock
you a dozen ways.

I believe he does the definitive version of my song "Gallo del Cielo."

AUGIE MEYERS *as* **Marshal and Evangelist Augie Blood**
(vocals: "He'll Be Dead Before He Hits The Ground" #1 and #2;
vocals, piano: "Just A Closer Walk [With Augie Blood]," "Rock of
Ages;" vocals, accordion: "Isn't It Grand?")
www.augiemeyers.com

American music legend Augie Meyers was born in San Antonio,
Texas in the '40s. In the early '60s, Augie and Doug Sahm founded
The Sir Douglas Quintet. Augie's Vox organ was a distinct element of the group's
sound on hits like: "She's About A Mover" (1964), "Mendocino" (1969), and "Nuevo
Laredo" (1970).

In the '90s, Augie co-founded the successful super group The Texas Tornados
with Doug Sahm, Flaco Jimenez, and Freddy Fender. Since the '70s, Augie has
written and recorded many original hits and has operated several of his own record
labels. He has recorded and toured with dozens of major acts, including Bob Dylan,
Tom Waits, and Jeff Bridges.

BARRY WALSH *as* **The Saloon Piano Man**
(piano—Nashville sessions; vocals: "This Is The Last Frontier/
Guilty" Chorus)
www.barrywalshmusic.com

Barry Walsh is one of the premier keyboard players working
out of Nashville. He has toured with Roy Orbison, Waylon Jennings,
Alex Chilton & The Box Tops, T.V. star Elizabeth McGovern, and
currently with his wife, Gretchen Peters. He is a fine producer and co-produced my
record *Mesabi*, and also has recorded three great solo piano records.

FATS KAPLIN *as* The Fiddlin' Fatman
(vocal intro and fiddle: "You Gotta Have A Dance;" accordion: "Gallo del Cielo;" pedal steel: Midnight Wine")
www.pulpcountry.com

Fats is a major American multi-instrumentalist. He plays fiddle, lap steel, and pedal steel on this record—but I've seen him perform on dozens of instruments, including Oud and Tex-Mex accordion. I first met Fats in the early 1980s in NYC. We had a band with Andrew Hardin and Billy Troiani that toured the East Coast, Canada, Norway, and Europe. Fats currently tours with Jack White, and has toured with many major rock and country acts. He is married to the great "pulp-country" singer Kristi Rose. They have several records out.

MOSES "CLEAR ROCK" PLATT
(vocals: "St. James Hospital")

Way out in West Texas, up on some hill!
    —Moses *"Clear Rock"* Platt, "St. James Hospital"

In the 1930s John and Alan Lomax tapped a goldmine of folklore in two African American prisoners at Central State Prison Farm in Sugar Land Texas—James "Iron Head" Baker and Moses "Clear Rock" Platt. Lomax had previously "discovered" Huddie Ledbetter, a.k.a. Lead Belly, in Angola prison in Louisiana, but Lead Belly and Lomax had a falling out.

Clear Rock (real name unknown) told the Lomaxes that he was given the name because he killed three people by throwing rocks at them. For that he was given a life sentence but he "got pardoned out." Then he "took up" with a young woman he described as a "li'l yeller gal." Moses was ignorant of the fact, he claimed, that she was only fourteen years old. He was recalled to serve his life sentence. When first recorded by the Lomaxes, in 1933, he was seventy-one years old, having spent forty-seven years in Texas prisons. He described himself as a habitual criminal.

Clear Rock was later pardoned by Texas' lady Governor Ferguson, by singing her a song. (That's how Lead Belly got out, or so goes the story.) Lomax said of Clear Rock: "He seemed to possess an endless body of songs. He also was something of a folklorist's dream as he knew any number of individual songs, and was able to make up several new ones on the spot. He never sang the same song twice."

Clear Rock sang an epic version of "The Old Chisholm Trail," with dozens of verses, which ended, according to Alan Lomax ". . . with the cowboy pitched off his pinto and lying hung in a mesquite tree." What we hear in his version of "St. James Hospital" is a variety of verses chopped out of cowboy songs and wrapped up into a spontaneous sort of rap performance. One of a kind song.

You can hear Clear Rock and Iron Head (and Lead Belly) on an excellent Rounder recording: *The Black Texicans,* consisting of some of the Lomaxes' field recordings in prisons. Hal Cannon, the great folklorist and singer, turned me on to this record. John Lomax also devoted a chapter to Clear Rock and Iron Head in his book: *The Ballad Hunter.*

JIMMY LAFAVE
(guitar and vocal: "Ain't No More Cane On The Brazos")
www.jimmylafave.com

One of the finest singer-songwriters on the Austin scene, Jimmy hails from Wills Point, Texas, a small town east of Dallas.

LaFave has dozens of fine roots records out and the focus is always on his voice. *True grit soul.* Jimmy is also one of the best interpreters of Bob Dylan songs. His voice seems to have all the elements of a great saxophone solo, sort of like Van Morrison.

CHIP TAYLOR and JOHN PLATANIA
(music: "The Last Running")
ww.trainwreckrecords.com
www.johnplatania.com

Chip Taylor and John Platania were kind enough to let me use their instrumental track "I Will Be Standing," which is from a Chip Taylor song. My friend John Jackson sent the music one time in one of his email newsletters, and I loved the piece and figured it would fit the lyrics I wrote about Charlie Goodnight's last buffalo run.

This music is off John Platania's record *Blues Waltzes and Badland Borders.* John has played guitar for Chip for many years and also toured with Van Morrison. Chip, of course, is a great songwriter—from "Wild Thing" and "Angel of the Morning" on down to the material on the dozens of fine records he's released in the last twenty years.

WALT WHITMAN
(recitation, "America")

Walt Whitman (May 31, 1819–March 26, 1892) was an American poet, essayist, and journalist. A humanist, Whitman is known as the father of free verse, and is one of our most influential poets. His work had a profound influence on Allen Ginsberg and the Beats in the 1950s. Whitman wandered through post-Civil War America and seemed to sing up the landscape. This is one of the only known wax recordings of his voice.

RAMBLIN' JACK ELLIOTT
(vocals: "The Sky Above, The Mud Below")

Did you ever stand and shiver, just because you were lookin' at a river?
  —Ramblin' Jack Elliott, "912 Greens"

It's fitting that Ramblin' Jack Elliott follows Walt Whitman. I consider them both on the same level as far as their influence on American poetry and music. Deep folk culture!

Ramblin' Jack was born Elliott Charles Adnopoz in Brooklyn New York, 1931, ran away from home and joined the rodeo and changed his name to Ramblin' Jack. He lived with Woody Guthrie, and took American folk and cowboy music back to Europe in the 1950s, where he busked on the streets of Rome, Paris, and London with Derroll Adams (who deserves also to be on this record.) Mick Jagger saw Jack busking on a subway platform and this influenced Mick to quit art school and become a singer.

Jack returned to Greenwich Village in the early 1960s and was a big influence on the early singing and guitar styles of young Bob Dylan. Jack is still out there on the road—a real died-in-the-wool troubadour—a great cowboy singer.

Jack's an American treasure, and was one of the best men (along with Ian Tyson) at my wedding in Elko, Nevada, to the lovely Nadine. Ramblin' Jack and Ian Tyson were huge influences on my work. Long Live Ramblin' Jack!

JACK HARDY and DAVID MASSENGILL

(performance: "The Road To Fairfax County")

www.davidmassengill.com

I met both these guys in the New York Village folk scene in the 1980s and '90s. Both were very active in keeping original folk music alive. Jack died recently—but he was a Village stalwart. David Massengill has written fine songs (I recorded his song: "Rider On An Orphan Train" on my record *The Man From God Knows Where*.) "On The Road to Fairfax County," is one of David's great songs—a fine version was recorded by The Roches. This cut is off the record *The Folk Brothers: Partners in Crime* by Jack Hardy and David Massengill on Great Divide records.

TEX RITTER

(vocals: "Blood on the Saddle")

There was blood on the saddle . . .
And blood all around . . . .

How could you have a horse opera without the voice of Tex Ritter? I consider Tex's LP *Blood on the Saddle*, along with Marty Robbins' *Gunfighter Ballads and Trail Songs,* and Ian Tyson's *Cowboyography,* to be the cornerstones of western music.

Woodward Maurice Ritter was born in 1905 Murvaul, Texas, and grew up on a farm in Panola county. He died in 1972 in Nashville. In between he made his mark as a lecturer, actor, cowboy singer and champion of western folklore. He even took a Wild West show to Europe.

As a teenager Tex yearned to be a lawyer, and he eventually entered the University of Texas. The law path didn't work out and Tex became focused on cowboy and western lore. J. Frank Dobie and John Lomax encouraged Tex to pursue a career in singing cowboy songs. That's Tex singing "High Noon" at the opening of that classic movie. Enough said.

A.L. "BERT" LLOYD

(vocals: "The Unfortunate Rake")

Albert Lancaster Lloyd (1908–1982) usually known as A.L. Lloyd or Bert Lloyd, was an English folk singer and collector of folk songs, and as was a key figure in the folk music revival of the 1950s and 1960s. He recorded at least six discs of Australian Bush ballads and folk music.

Lloyd had an amazing and prolific career—he worked as a sheep shearer in Australia and aboard whaling ships in the Antarctic—keeping his ear cocked for folk songs. He can be seen singing a sea shanty in the John Huston film *Moby Dick*.

On this record he sings "The Unfortunate Rake," which is a precursor to "The Streets of Laredo." Lloyd ranks alongside Francis James Child, Cecil Sharp, Ewan MacColl, Ralph Vaughn Williams, John Lomax, and Howard Thorpe as pioneers in folk song collecting.

FINBAR FUREY

(vocals and Uilleann pipes: "Carrickfergus")

www.finbarfurey.com

In the early 1990s I was in a pub in York, England, in mid-afternoon sitting there at the bar eating lunch when Eric Bogle's great anti-war song "The Green Fields of France" came on the jukebox and spilled out over the empty room. The song is a big one. Devastating lyrics.

But it was the singer who was wrenching the heart and blood out of the lyric—the singer pulled me into the story. Grabbed me by the throat. The Irish singer Finbar Furey. He remains one of my favorite singers, along with Ana Gabriel and Maura O'Connell, and it is indeed a deep honor to have the three voices on this record.

Finbar was born in Dublin, into a heritage of traveling musicians. His father Ted taught Finbar the Uilleann pipes at an early age and Finbar became a renowned piper and also plays banjo, guitar, and tin whistle. Early on he formed The Fureys with his brothers Eddie, Paul, and George—one of the most successful groups in Ireland.

Finbar now has a successful solo career and many fine recent albums. He has also appeared in films such as Scorsese's "Gangs of New York." This is a voice that could never lie. An Irish voice for sure.

SOURDOUGH SLIM
(performance: "The Fairground Pugilist")
www.sourdoughslim.com

One of the most original and beloved Western entertainers. Sourdough Slim, transports us to a old time world where vaudevillian camp and cowboy lore intermingle.

    Slim, a.k.a. Rick Crowder, is a well traveled veteran of stages ranging from The National Cowboy Poetry Gathering to The Lincoln Center's Roots of American Music Festival and the Carnegie Hall Folk Festival. His fast-paced stage show finds him crooning Western classics, playing accordion, guitar and harmonica, dancing a jig, dishing out hilarious comedic sketches and letting loose with mind boggling yodeling. As Ian Tyson has stated: Slim is the best physical comedian around.

COWBOY VOICES BEYOND THE CAMPFIRE:

KEVIN "BLACKIE" FARRELL wrote one of the classic "turn of the screw" cowboy songs of all time, "Sonora's Death Row." It's been an influence on me—and kept me away from drinking *mescal*. Blackie's written dozens of classic cowboy, folk, country, and rockabilly songs. Commander Cody and Bill Kirchen have recorded a lot of Blackie's material.

ROSS KNOX is a muleteer and cowboy poet *par excellence*. For years he packed mules down into the Grand Canyon every morning and was involved in many mule wrecks over the years. He now packs into Yosemite National Park. Here he sings the old chestnut: "I'm The Man Who Rode the Mule Around the World." I wrote about Ross in an essay in *Ranch and Reata* magazine—the finest journal in the West. **www.ranchandreata.com**

GLEN ORHLIN ("Old Desert Sands") is a cowboy, bronc rider, folklorist, raconteur, and singer who now ranches in Arkansas. Glenn has many great cowboy records out and published a collection of cowboy songs: *The Hellbound Train.*

PAT RUSSELL is my older brother—he left L.A. in the '50s, horseback, and never looked back. Bull rider, Bronc Rider, steer wrestler, horseshoer, rancher . . . currently major livestock contractor in California. I learned my first cowboy songs from my brother and his vast record collection and I stole his Tijuana guitar 'cause he couldn't carry a tune. Here he recites the first verse to "The Castration of the Strawberry Roan." The rest is fairly unprintable. We co-authored an essay on horses in the L.A. Basin in *Ranch and Reata.*

JOHN TRUDELL

(performance: "Crazy Horse")

www.johntrudell.com

John Trudell (Santee Sioux) is an American author, poet, actor, musician. He was the spokesperson for the United Indians All Tribes Takeover of Alcatraz beginning in 1969, broadcasting as Radio Free Alcatraz. During most of the 1970s, he served as the chairman of the American Indian Movement. John is one of our finest American poets. I first met him in Italy, where we both were performing in an open air concert in a city square. I find his words and performances intense and imbued with courage and passion. This performance of his poem "Crazy Horse" is off the 2002 album *Bone Days* produced by actress Angelina Jolie. The Native voice chanting is Quiltman.

THAD BECKMAN

(guitars: "The Water Is Wide;" performance: "Custer's Luck")

www.thadbeckman.com

Thad Beckman has been backing me up on guitar for the last six years or so. He's an accomplished American guitarist, with CDs and books out, and a helluva songwriter with deep interest in the history of the American West. He was raised in Oregon and now lives in Denver. This man has mastered American fingerpicking blues style guitar. His CDs are available through his website.

HENRY REAL BIRD (vocals: "The Door Song")

Henry is a Crow Indian poet who grew up near the Custer Battleground up there in the Badlands. You can hear him chanting "The Door Song" in the distance in the collage of crow and wolf sounds that weave into "Crazy Horse" by John Trudell.

❧ ACT TWO ❧

MAURA O'CONNELL *as* Rose Malloy

(vocals: "The Water Is Wide," "I Talk To God," "The Rose of Roscrae")

www.mauraoconnell.com

A lot of people think every singer is someone's puppet, that they are not fully invested in the song — that they are at the whim of a producer or a songwriter or a band. Singing has been denigrated like that for too long. —Maura O'Connell

Maura O'Connell was born in Ennis, the main town in Country Clare, in the West of Ireland. Her mother's family owned Costello's Fish Shop in Ennis where Maura worked, until music became her full-time career. She grew up listening to her mother's light opera, opera, and parlor song records. Her father loved Irish rebel ballads.

She began her professional musical journey during a six-week tour of the US in 1980, as vocalist for the traditionally based Celtic group De Dannan. The following year, she was featured on the band's landmark album, *The Star Spangled Molly*, which became a national phenomenon in Ireland.

Maura moved to the US in 1986, to Nashville. She's since recorded a slew of highly acclaimed and Grammy nominated records. The 2009 album *Naked With Friends*, is Maura's first *a cappella* album. Aside from the music world, Martin Scorsese cast Maura as an Irish migrant street singer in his 19th century epic *The Gangs of New York,* released in 2002.

Maura's voice cuts deep into the roots of a song and resonates with Irish soul.

ELIZA GILKYSON

(vocals: "The Bear," "Jesus Met The Woman At The Well;" guitar, vocals: "The Railroad Boy")

www.elizagilkyson.com

Eliza's father was a great folk based songwriter, Terry Gilkyson, who wrote "Fast Freight," "Marianne," and other classics, along with songs for many Walt Disney films. Eliza has recorded dozens of albums laced with her deep, well-crafted original songs—one of the strongest writers to consistently release fresh music with new insights. She also possesses and edgy, no bullshit voice which refuses to lie to you.

THE MCCRARY SISTERS

(backing vocals: "Resurrection Mountain")

I worked with the McCrary's on my *Mesabi* record and got to hear all their great stories about working with Bob Dylan during his Gospel years. They come from church music and are still deeply involved with Gospel singing in the Nashville area.

GRETCHEN PETERS

www.gretchenpeters.com

(vocals: "This Is The Last Frontier/Guilty," "Ain't No More Cane On The Brazos," "When The Wolves No Longer Sing," "Tularosa," "The Rose of Roscrae;" vocals, guitar: "Guadalupe")

As I write this Gretchen Peters was just inducted into the Nashville Songwriter's Hall of Fame. I got to know Gretchen after writing a fan letter to her when I heard her record: *Halcyon*. We became friends and a made a record on the West: *One to the Heart, One to the Head*. This is a big time writer. She's written a slew of top ten hits including *"Independence Day"* and *"Bus to St. Cloud,"* and co-written songs with Bryan Adams. She never cops out to commerciality. She makes commerciality come to her own deep vision. And kneel down.

ANA GABRIEL

(vocals: "Valentine de la Sierra")

What can you say? If Finbar Furey and Maura O'Connell are the voices of Ireland, then Ana Gabriel is the voice of Mexico.

This is a big-hearted singer. She rips the flesh off of this old *corrido* and throws it into your lap. I first heard her on a jukebox in Juarez and I never got over it. For a great dose of Ana Gabriel check out the DVD (on YouTube) *Live in the Mexico City Bull Ring*. To have Ana, Finbar and Maura on the same record is a gift from God.

IAN TYSON

(vocals: "Gallo del Cielo")

www.iantyson.com

Ian Tyson has probably been the biggest influence on me as a singer-songwriter. I grew up listening to Ian and Sylvia (no doubt the strongest folk group to emerge from the '60s), and later became his friend when he recorded my song "Gallo del Cielo" on his first cowboy record: *Old Corrals and Sagebrush*.

Ian wrote "Four Strong Winds," the most popular song ever written in Canada, and also the cowboy classic *Someday Soon*.

He's written at least 100 great songs, and I credit him with single-handedly resurrecting the cowboy song movement in the 1980s. He's still going strong at age 81, as I write this. We co-wrote "When the Wolves No Longer Sing" for this record and have ideas for other new songs. Ian and I also co-wrote "Navajo Rug," "Claude Dallas," "The Rose of San Joaquin," and others.

There is not enough space here to carve out the magnitude of debt myself (and all of American Folk and Cowboy Music) owe Ian Tyson. I came out of those same bars he did on Skid Row in British Columbia and I consider him a blood brother in song.

SWISS YODEL CHOIR

I snuck up behind these folks who were singing on a mountain top during Swiss Independence Day in 2014. I tried to sing a bass part and blend in, and they allowed it. This form of yodeling goes back hundred of years. Echoes off the alps. Swiss and German folks settled in different parts of Texas. The yodel was picked up by singing cowboys back in the 1920s and '30s. Yodel is still popular in Switzerland today.

BONNIE DOBSON

(performance: "En Canadiene Errant")

I was performing in London, at the Cecil Sharp Center, when someone told me Bonnie Dobson was in the audience.

I never got to meet her in person—but I was honored and we now write letters back and forth. Bonnie is Canadian (we need Canadian music on this record!) and was a fixture in the Village folk scene in the '60s. In fact, Bob Dylan mentioned that some of her songs were an influence on him. She wrote the folk classic "Morning Dew." Bonnie moved to England years ago and is still actively performing and recording.

LEAD BELLY

(performance: "When I Was A Cowboy" a.k.a. "Western Cowboy")

He called himself "The King of the 12-String Guitar" and his full name was Huddie William Ledbetter (1888–1949). In January 1918 he was imprisoned at the Imperial Farm in Sugar Land, Texas, after killing one of his relatives, Will Stafford, in a fight over a woman. There he may have first heard the traditional prison song "Midnight Special." Later he went on to compose his big song, "Goodnight Irene."

In 1930 Ledbetter was in Angola Prison Farm in Louisiana after a summary trial for attempted homicide, charged with stabbing a white man in a fight. He was "discovered" there three years later during a visit by folklorists John and Alan Lomax. The Lomaxes returned to record Lead Belly several times. Lead Belly later received a pardon by singing for the governor of Louisiana. Lead Belly became a fixture inn the Village and published a book of folk songs. He worked for Lomax for awhile but they eventually had a bitter falling out over money.

GUY CLARK (vocals: "Desperados Waiting for a Train")
www.guyclark.com

Guy Clark, from Monahans, Texas, is a guitar builder, a painter, and a master songwriter. I don't need to detail all of his great ones, but I like to paint pictures out here in West Texas listening to Guy Clark. He summons up the landscape. *Magic.* The morning I spent with him recently in Nashville—recording a few verses of this song, was one of the most moving moments of my life. Like swapping yarns with Picasso on the edge of Barcelona. He had West Texas in his eyes. I think of this song every time I drive across Texas. He's one of the greats.

DAN PENN
(vocals: Desperados Waiting for a Train")
www.danpenn.com

Dan Penn really nailed the vocal on this one. Dan co-wrote "Do Right Woman, Do Right Man" and "The Dark End of the Street" with Chips Moman, and also wrote hit songs with Spooner Oldham. He's still writing classics. Dan is responsible for a great many soul and country hits. He is also a record producer, fan of old junkyard cars, and is considered one of the finest white soul singers of our time.

GURF MORLIX
(bass, guitars: "The Bear," "Jesus Met The Woman At The Well;" bass, vocals: "Isn't It Grand?")

Gurf Morlix produced one of my earlier records, *Borderland*, and is a revered multi-instrumentalist and songwriter living on the edge of Austin, Texas. Gurf toured with Lucinda Williams, Warren Zevon, and Harry Dean Stanton, and produced dozens of great Austin songwriter records and now records his own original records and tours as a solo.

PAT MANSKE
(drums: "The Bear," "Jesus Met The Woman At The Well;" vocals: "Isn't It Grand?")

I met Pat while he was playing drums for The Flatlanders. He plays drums on several of these tracks, sings on "Isn't it Grand?" and also engineered the tracks record at The Zone recording studio in Dripping Springs, Texas.

Epilogue:
If This Had Been
Enough of A Record

If this had been enough of a book it would have had everything in it . . . the great thing is to last and get your work done and write when there is something that you know, and not before . . . then any part that you make will represent the whole if it's made truly . . .
 —Ernest Hemingway, *Death in the Afternoon*

My favorite piece of Hemingway's writing is the last chapter of *Death in the Afternoon,* in which he includes a hundred small scenes and anecdotes which didn't make the main body of the work. It's masterful writing and is drenched in deep nostalgia for the beauty of the Spain, a country which the Old Man loved. He is saddened by the parts he left out of the book, then nods towards them. He is masterful in the nodding. The old man also said, in his Nobel Prize acceptance speech:

> (A writer) does his work alone and if he is a good enough writer he must face
> eternity, or the lack of it, each day . . . It is because we have had such great writers
> in the past that a writer is driven far out past where he can go, out to where no
> one can help him.

This record was certainly heading far out past where I thought it could go. It's on it's own now, like a child that leaves your hearth and ventures out to become President, or a horse thief. There are many roads.

But, if this had been enough of a record it would have included Camaron de la Isla singing his *cante hondo,* with that soulful, scratchy, junkie voice. When he died there were 100,00 people at his funeral in Cadiz. *Deep song,* the bed rock of cowboy music, echoing back to Andalucia.

I should have had mariachis singing in the marketplace, and *paso dobles* from the Juarez bull ring band, and *Oomp Pa Pa* polka bands from central Texas, and Marty Robbins singing "El Paso" on the jukebox at Rosa's Cantina in El Paso (at happy hour), and I could have done with a lot more of Anna Gabriel, Ramblin' Jack Elliott, and Ian Tyson.

And Don Edwards should have been on here, and Buck Ramsey, and Katie Lee singing "10,000 Goddamn Cattle" into my telephone recently—90 years of age and going strong—and Hedy West and Karen Dalton with their banjos, I had to cut that part out. And what about Rosalie Sorrels singing "My Last Go Round?" *If only.* And there were many more Eliza Gilkyson songs, great verses from tradition, that had to go.

I should have included Casey Tibbs' final soliloquy and advice to young bronc riders: *you don't leave home for second place.* I have it on tape somewhere. ī could have done with a hell of a lot more of Henry Real Bird (Crow) and John Trudell (Santee

Sioux), and for that matter Peter La Farge should have been on here singing "The Ballad of Ira Hayes" or one of his cowboy songs. Yes, and Harry Jackson. And Patsy Montana and Bob Wills and every singing cowboy from the 1930s to the '50s. And Sonny Rollins blowing jazz saxophone on his "Western" album *Way Out West*.

And at one point, since this story begins with a hanging, I was going to end it all in 1958 with the Kingston Trio singing "Tom Dooley" (for cultural balance!), a hanging song that sold millions of records. Just to prove a point. I had the rights to one of the live recordings, but I couldn't fit it all, and both sides of the record were running well over the proscribed 78 minutes—the engineers and fellow producers were casting strange glances in my direction.

It could have been a ten record set—but we live at a time when most folks have forgotten about albums filled with two sides of music and lots of songs. (*What's happened to our music? Where have the wild ones gone?*)

Where are the stampedes, the clatter of hooves, the western swing dance bands, and cowboy yodeling? We needed more shootouts and a hell of a lot more Tex Ritter.

But all that's left, to quote Papa Hemingway, is to present a small piece of it, the part you know, so that listeners might dream up the thing as a whole. *The West of the imagination.* That small portion you show is the tip of the iceberg. But I've rambled on enough. It's the music that counts.

God bless the music and the voices that bring the music into our hearts.

—Tom Russell
El Paso, Texas, October 2014

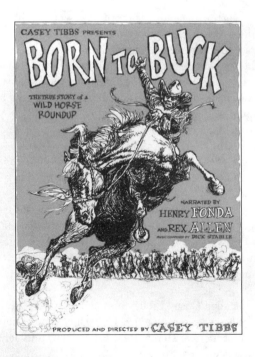